"To my amazing wife, a brilliant product owner and software team manager, whose leadership and support have been my guiding light throughout this journey. And to my daughter, with her sharp engineering and logical mindset, who inspires me every day. Your love and encouragement have made writing this book a truly wonderful experience."

The Tale of the Floating Garden

In a distant land surrounded by endless waters, a community of islanders dreamed of building a **floating garden**—a sanctuary where life could thrive amidst the vast ocean. The garden would be a place of growth, harmony, and innovation, capable of expanding and adapting as the community's needs evolved.

At first, each group of islanders began working on their own piece of the garden. Some focused on growing lush greenery, while others built wooden walkways or water filtration systems. But as the pieces came together, problems emerged. The walkways didn't align, the plants wilted in areas without proper irrigation, and the filtration systems clogged because they weren't designed to handle the load.

The garden, though ambitious, teetered on the edge of collapse.

The Visionary Plan

Amidst the chaos, a wise elder named Auru stepped forward. She had spent years observing the ocean's rhythms and the balance of life. "This floating garden cannot thrive on isolated efforts," she said. "It needs a **living framework**, a structure that unites our ideas and adapts to the shifting tides."

Auru's vision was simple yet profound:

The Foundation: A sturdy, interconnected base that could float steadily, carrying the weight of all future additions.

The Ecosystem: Modules for each purpose—gardens for food, channels for water, and platforms for gathering—that were designed to connect seamlessly.

The Flow: Clear pathways and pipelines ensuring that resources like sunlight, water, and nutrients flowed freely to all parts of the garden.

Auru didn't dictate the details but created **guiding principles** that allowed each group to innovate within a shared vision. She also ensured the garden could evolve—parts could be removed, expanded, or replaced without disrupting the whole.

What Happened Next

Under Auru's guidance, the floating garden flourished. The plants thrived, the walkways expanded effortlessly, and the filtration systems scaled with the community's growth. More importantly, the garden became a living organism, resilient to storms and adaptable to the ocean's changes.

The Floating Garden as Software Architecture

This floating garden is a metaphor for software systems, and Auru's guiding principles represent **software architecture**. Just as Auru designed a framework to unite and sustain the garden, a software architect creates a foundation that ensures a system's components work harmoniously. The garden's modular parts mirror software modules, while the pathways resemble data flows and communication protocols.

The beauty of Auru's approach was its adaptability. Similarly, software architecture ensures that systems can grow and evolve without falling apart, enabling resilience, scalability, and seamless functionality.

By the end of this book, you'll be equipped to design your own "floating gardens" in the digital world—software systems that thrive in any environment.

Introduction

What is the hidden thought from the previous story? Despite advancements in technology and methodologies, many projects still falter, leaving teams frustrated and stakeholders disillusioned. This book takes you on a comprehensive journey to explore the common pitfalls that lead to software project failures and, more importantly, to uncover the strategies that can turn these challenges into triumphs.

Throughout these pages, we will delve into the key reasons behind software project failures, from unclear requirements and poor communication to insufficient testing and lack of stakeholder engagement. Each chapter will not only highlight these pitfalls but will also provide actionable insights and proven methodologies to help you navigate the complexities of software development.

By the end of this journey, you will be equipped with a robust toolkit of best practices, innovative approaches, and a deep understanding of what it takes to create successful software projects. Whether you are a seasoned developer, a project manager, or a curious newcomer to the software world, this book aims to empower you with the knowledge and confidence to deliver exceptional results in your projects. Join us as we embark on this exploration and discover the keys to transforming software challenges into opportunities for success.

Famous software projects that failed

Toyota's Vehicle Recall Due to Software Issues (2010)
Project: Toyota's attempt to introduce advanced vehicle control systems that included electronic throttle control.

Architectural Issues: The vehicle's software architecture lacked redundancy and fault tolerance, making it vulnerable to malfunction. This became especially apparent when acceleration issues arose.

Outcome: The system failures led to a massive recall, lawsuits, and billions of dollars in damages, exposing flaws in the architecture that prioritized efficiency over safety.

Lufthansa's Airline Booking System (2010)
Project: A system overhaul for Lufthansa's flight booking and ticketing platform.

Architectural Issues: The new architecture couldn't scale with the increasing volume of bookings, and its monolithic design made it hard to modify or fix. This inflexibility led to frequent crashes and system slowdowns during peak booking times.

Outcome: The poor architecture cost Lufthansa millions in lost bookings and customer dissatisfaction, prompting a costly re-architecture of the system.

MySpace Revamp (2013)
Project: A redesign of the once-popular social networking site to regain users and compete with Facebook.

Architectural Issues: The new architecture was overly complex and unable to handle the legacy data from the old site. Additionally, the user experience was hindered by the slow load times and complicated navigation.

Outcome: The revamped MySpace failed to attract a significant user base, leading to its decline as a social media platform.

Adobe Flash Player (2010s)
Project: A multimedia software platform for creating animations, web applications, and video content.

Architectural Issues: Flash suffered from security vulnerabilities and performance issues due to its complex architecture and reliance on outdated technology. The architecture became a target for exploits, leading to significant security breaches.

Outcome: Adobe officially ended support for Flash Player in 2020 due to its decline and the move towards more secure technologies like HTML.

What did all of them have in common?

The failed projects listed share several common characteristics that contributed to their challenges and ultimate failures. Here are the key similarities:

Poor Architectural Decisions
Many of the projects suffered from overly complex or inadequate architectural designs that could not scale, integrate, or adapt to the project's evolving needs.

Lack of Stakeholder Engagement

Insufficient involvement of key stakeholders during the planning and execution phases often led to misunderstandings of requirements and a misalignment between project goals and user needs.

Inadequate Requirement Analysis

A failure to thoroughly analyze and document requirements often resulted in systems that did not meet user expectations or address real-world challenges.

Integration Challenges

Many projects struggled with integrating new systems with existing infrastructure or legacy systems, leading to inefficiencies and delays.

Scope Creep and Ambitious Goals

Overly ambitious project scopes and failure to manage changes effectively often resulted in projects that became unmanageable and costly.

Poor Project Management

Weak project management practices, including inadequate risk management and lack of monitoring, contributed to delays, cost overruns, and eventual project failure.

Lack of Testing and Quality Assurance

Insufficient testing and quality control often resulted in undetected issues that could have been addressed early, leading to significant problems during deployment.

Technological Incompatibility

Many projects attempted to utilize outdated or incompatible technologies, leading to performance issues and difficulties in maintaining the systems.

Failure to Adapt to User Needs

Many projects did not evolve based on user feedback, resulting in solutions that did not align with user expectations or practical use cases.

Budget Overruns and Financial Mismanagement
Cost overruns were common in many projects, often leading to delays and scope reductions.

This frequently resulted in projects being scrapped or significantly restructured due to financial constraints. As a result, resources were often diverted to other priorities, further escalating the challenges. The need for better budgeting and financial oversight became increasingly apparent in ensuring the completion of these projects.

Lack of Clear Vision or Objectives
Many projects lacked a clear, cohesive vision or set of objectives, making it difficult for teams to align their efforts effectively.

Resistance to Change
Organizational resistance to adopting new technologies or processes often hindered the successful implementation of the projects.

Summary

These common factors highlight the importance of careful planning, effective communication, stakeholder involvement, and robust architectural design in ensuring the success of software projects. Addressing these issues early in the project lifecycle can significantly enhance the likelihood of successful outcomes.

The Cost of Complexity: The Importance of Clear Architecture in Software Projects

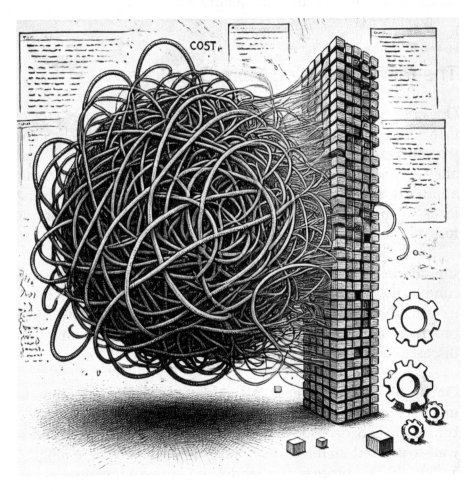

In software development, complexity is often viewed as an unavoidable aspect of projects. Teams deal with intricate codebases, convoluted dependencies, and evolving requirements. However, a key yet overlooked factor contributing to this complexity is the lack of clear architectural structure and design principles. When architecture lacks clarity and alignment with essential qualities, it leads to issues that impact timelines, budgets, and overall software quality.

The Pitfall of Adding More Developers

One of the most common responses to an overly complex project is to simply throw more developers at the problem. The belief is that increasing the team size will accelerate progress and alleviate the burden of a complex codebase. Unfortunately, this approach often backfires. The **myth of "adding more hands"** leads to increased short-term and long-term costs in various forms:

Communication Overhead: As team size grows, so does the complexity of communication. More developers mean more meetings, updates, and coordination efforts. This can slow down progress significantly, as developers spend more time on discussions rather than actual coding.

Onboarding Challenges: New developers need time to understand the existing system, its architecture, and the rationale behind design decisions. Without clear documentation and a well-structured architecture, onboarding can become a lengthy and frustrating process, further delaying project timelines.

Increased Risk of Errors: A larger team can lead to inconsistencies in coding practices and architectural understanding. Without a cohesive vision, developers may introduce bugs or create code that conflicts with existing structures, increasing the maintenance burden.

Diminished Morale: When developers are faced with a complex, poorly designed system, frustration can lead to decreased morale. High turnover rates often ensue, compounding the challenges associated with onboarding and knowledge transfer.

The Case for Quality Architecture

Rather than simply increasing the number of developers to combat complexity, a more effective solution is to invest in high-quality architecture. This involves designing systems with architectural qualities in mind, such as:

Clarity: A well-defined architecture provides a clear understanding of system components, their interactions, and their purposes. This clarity reduces cognitive load for developers, allowing them to focus on building features rather than deciphering code.

Modularity: A modular architecture promotes separation of concerns, enabling teams to work on individual components independently. This reduces interdependencies, making it easier to add new features or make changes without affecting the entire system.

Scalability: Designing with scalability in mind ensures that the system can grow with user demands. A well-architected system can accommodate increased loads without a complete redesign, reducing future costs.

Testability: Clear architecture allows for better testing practices. When components are well-defined and decoupled, writing tests becomes easier, leading to improved software quality and reduced bug-related costs.

Maintainability: High-quality architecture simplifies maintenance. When the codebase is structured logically, developers can make changes more easily, resulting in lower long-term costs associated with bug fixes and feature additions.

Long-Term Cost Benefits
Investing in a clear architectural framework may seem like a significant upfront cost, but the long-term benefits often far outweigh these initial investments. Some of the cost benefits include:

Reduced Time to Market: With a clear architecture, teams can develop features more rapidly. The time spent on onboarding new developers decreases, and the reduced complexity allows for quicker decision-making.

Lower Maintenance Costs: A well-structured system is easier to maintain and update. As a result, the costs associated with fixing bugs and implementing changes are minimized, freeing up resources for innovation.

Enhanced Developer Productivity: Developers can work more effectively when they understand the system architecture and have access to clear guidelines. This leads to higher job satisfaction and reduces turnover rates.

Improved Customer Satisfaction: A system designed with quality architecture can respond better to customer needs, resulting in a more reliable and enjoyable user experience. Happier customers often lead to increased sales and better brand loyalty.

Conclusion

The temptation to **address project complexity by simply adding more developers** can lead to **increased costs and inefficiencies** in the long run. Instead, investing in a clear and well-structured architecture designed with architectural qualities in mind is crucial for fostering a successful software project. By prioritizing clarity, modularity, scalability, testability, and maintainability, organizations can significantly reduce both short-term and long-term costs while improving overall software quality. Embracing the value of high-quality architecture not only benefits the project but also empowers development teams to thrive in a complex software landscape.

The Hidden Costs of Unskilled Developers in Software Projects

The temptation to hire unskilled or junior developers at a lower hourly rate can be enticing for organizations looking to manage budgets. However, this approach can often lead to significantly higher expenses in the long run. While it may seem economical at first, relying on less experienced developers can create a range of challenges that ultimately inflate project costs and compromise quality.

Is quality a cost?

The principle of "you get what you pay for" is particularly relevant in software development. Skilled developers bring not only technical expertise but also experience, problem-solving capabilities, and a deeper understanding of best practices. Here are several compelling reasons why investing in highly skilled software experts can lead to more cost-effective and successful projects:

Higher Productivity: Experienced developers can work more efficiently, producing higher-quality code in less time. Their familiarity with various tools, frameworks, and languages allows them to avoid common pitfalls, expediting development processes and saving both time and resources.

Reduced Debugging and Maintenance Costs: Skilled developers excel at writing clean, maintainable code, which minimizes bugs and the need for extensive debugging. In contrast, less experienced developers may produce code that is more prone to errors, resulting in increased maintenance efforts and costs over time.

Better Design and Architecture: Experienced developers understand the importance of sound software architecture and can design systems that are scalable, flexible, and easy to maintain. Poor architectural decisions made by unskilled developers can lead to complex, tangled codebases that are difficult and expensive to modify in the future.

Effective Problem Solving: Skilled developers can anticipate potential issues and identify solutions proactively, preventing costly delays. Less experienced developers may struggle to troubleshoot problems, resulting in extended downtimes and project setbacks.

Enhanced Collaboration and Communication: Senior developers often possess strong interpersonal skills, enabling them to communicate effectively with team members, stakeholders, and clients. This leads to better collaboration and a clearer understanding of project requirements, reducing the risk of miscommunication that can result in costly rework.

The Cost of Managing Inexperienced Developers

In addition to the direct challenges associated with less experienced developers, there are indirect costs related to team dynamics and management. Unskilled developers often require a more complex team structure, resulting in increased management overhead. This can manifest in several ways:

Higher Management Needs: A larger team may be necessary to support inexperienced developers, leading to increased costs for project management, coordination, and alignment meetings. The time spent in sync meetings can detract from productive coding time, further slowing progress.

Pair Programming and Duplication of Effort: To mitigate risks associated with inexperience, organizations may need to implement pair programming or require multiple developers to collaborate on tasks. This can lead to duplicate efforts and inefficiencies, ultimately driving up costs.

Increased Investment in Validation and Verification: Given that less experienced developers may not always produce reliable code, additional resources must be allocated for testing and validation. This added layer of scrutiny can significantly increase project timelines and expenses.

Talent Retention Challenges: Once trained, there is a risk that unskilled developers may choose to pursue opportunities elsewhere, leading to higher turnover rates and the associated costs of onboarding new team members. This cycle can create further instability within a project.

The Impact of Team Composition

When considering the broader implications of team composition, it's essential to recognize the benefits of a smaller number of experienced developers, particularly in the context of remote and distributed teams. Collaborating with a diverse team from different cultural backgrounds can enhance creativity and innovation. However, this approach can also lead to complications:

Increased Team Size and Complexity: Relying on remote teams from varying cultures may necessitate a larger team structure to account for diverse skills and expertise, effectively doubling or tripling the size of the team required to achieve the same results as a few local experts.

Coordination Challenges: Managing a larger, geographically dispersed team can lead to coordination challenges, where time zones, communication styles, and work ethics must be harmonized. This complexity can further increase costs and lead to inefficiencies.

Conclusion

The choice to hire unskilled developers at a lower hourly rate may appear to be a cost-saving strategy, but the long-term implications can significantly outweigh any initial savings. While organizations may save money upfront, they risk incurring higher costs through increased management efforts, prolonged project timelines, and reduced software quality.

Investing in a smaller number of experienced developers — whether locally or within a distributed team — can lead to more efficient processes, better-quality outcomes, and ultimately greater overall satisfaction for both developers and clients. By prioritizing expertise and experience, organizations can ensure that their software projects are completed on time, within budget, and to a high standard of quality. In the end, choosing skilled developers is not merely an expense; it is a strategic decision that pays dividends in the success of software projects.

"Wow, who did this work before?"

When fixing plumbing or electrical systems, we rely on skilled tradespeople for their expertise. Similarly, organizations turn to software architects to navigate complex legacy systems. Despite working in different domains, both tradespeople and software architects share common approaches. This article explores the contrasting perspectives of plumbers, electricians, and software architects, focusing on the challenges, methodologies, and communication styles involved.

The Initial Assessment

The Tradesperson's Approach

When you call a plumber or electrician to fix issues in your home, the first step is usually an assessment. A plumber might say:

"Let's take a look at your pipes to identify the problem. We'll need to check for leaks and any clogs that could be causing issues. Depending on what we find, we may need to replace some sections or adjust the layout to ensure proper flow."

This initial assessment is critical for several reasons:

Identification of Symptoms: The tradesperson examines visible signs of problems, such as water stains, leaks, or flickering lights.

Diagnosis: They consider potential underlying issues that may not be immediately apparent, such as corrosion in pipes or outdated electrical circuits.

Communication: They often use layman's terms, ensuring homeowners understand the problem without overwhelming them with technical jargon.

The Software Architect's Approach

In contrast, when a software architect joins a legacy software project, their assessment may sound like:

"I need to review the existing architecture and codebase to understand the current system's capabilities and limitations. We'll analyze how various components interact and identify any technical debt that needs addressing."

This assessment involves different aspects:

Code Review: The architect delves into the code to understand its structure, dependencies, and potential issues.

Stakeholder Interviews: They engage with stakeholders to gather insights about user needs and expectations.

System Mapping: They create diagrams to visualize how different modules and components interact within the software ecosystem.

Understanding the Challenges

Challenges Faced by Tradespeople
When a plumber or electrician assesses a problem, they encounter various challenges:

Hidden Issues: Often, the problems are not immediately visible. A plumber might discover hidden leaks or blockages behind walls that complicate the repair process.

Code Compliance: Electricians must ensure their work adheres to local codes and regulations, which can limit their solutions and require additional adjustments.

Client Expectations: Homeowners may have certain expectations regarding timelines and costs, which can be challenging to manage.

Challenges Faced by Software Architects

Similarly, software architects face distinct challenges in legacy software projects:

Legacy Code: They often have to work with poorly documented or outdated code that lacks modern design principles, making it challenging to understand and modify.

Integration: Existing systems may rely on outdated technologies or frameworks, complicating integration efforts with modern solutions.

Changing Requirements: Stakeholder expectations may shift over time, requiring architects to adapt their solutions rapidly to accommodate new needs.

Proposed Solutions

Solutions from Tradespeople
After assessing the situation, a plumber or electrician might propose solutions such as:

"To fix the leak, we can replace the damaged pipe section and install a valve for easier access in the future. This will improve your plumbing system's efficiency."

Practical Fixes: Tradespeople provide straightforward, actionable solutions tailored to the specific problem.

Preventative Measures: They often recommend preventative measures, such as regular maintenance checks, to avoid future issues.

Cost Estimates: They provide clear estimates for labor and materials, allowing homeowners to make informed decisions.

Solutions from Software Architects

Conversely, a software architect might suggest:

"We should refactor the critical components of the legacy system and consider migrating to a microservices architecture. This will enhance scalability and maintainability while addressing current performance issues."

Strategic Planning: Software architects emphasize long-term strategies that align with business goals, focusing on system architecture and design.

Iterative Development: They often advocate for an agile approach, promoting continuous improvement and adaptation.
Documentation: Architects prioritize creating comprehensive documentation to facilitate future development and maintenance.

Communication Styles

Communication of Tradespeople
The communication style of tradespeople is generally straightforward and practical. They often emphasize clarity and use analogies or metaphors to help homeowners understand complex concepts. For example:

"Think of your plumbing system like your circulatory system. If there's a blockage, blood can't flow properly, leading to bigger issues."

This kind of analogy helps demystify the technical aspects of their work and fosters trust with clients.

Communication of Software Architects

In contrast, software architects may adopt a more technical communication style, especially when dealing with engineers and developers. They might say:

"We need to address the coupling and cohesion of the components to improve maintainability and reduce the risk of introducing bugs during future updates."

While their language can be more technical, successful architects make an effort to explain concepts in layman's terms to stakeholders who may not be as technically savvy. They may also use visual aids, such as diagrams and flowcharts, to convey complex ideas effectively.

Conclusion

In summary, both tradespeople and software architects face unique challenges and employ distinct methodologies in their respective fields. While tradespeople focus on immediate, practical fixes to physical systems, software architects address complex, long-term architectural concerns in software development. Both roles require effective communication, a thorough understanding of systems, and the ability to propose viable solutions to meet client needs.

Ultimately, whether fixing a leaky pipe or redesigning a legacy software system, the underlying principles of assessment, problem-solving, and effective communication remain fundamental to achieving successful outcomes. Understanding the perspectives of both tradespeople and software architects can provide valuable insights into how best to approach problem-solving across diverse domains.

Now let's do **the right thing** right.
What is the right thing to build?

The Pitfalls of Jumping to Code: A Call for Holistic Software Development

The rapid pace of software development often makes the temptation to jump straight into coding almost irresistible. Developers, **driven by excitement and the desire to create**, often find themselves **focusing on partial sunny-day scenarios** — ideal conditions under which their code will function perfectly.

And isn't this the MVP approach? However, this tendency to get lost in the minutiae of implementation can lead to significant misalignments with the overall project goals and stakeholder needs. This article explores the dangers of this approach, emphasizes the importance of understanding the big picture, and advocates for a more structured and stakeholder-centric approach to software development.

The Temptation of Immediate Implementation

The Allure of Coding

For many developers, the act of coding represents a form of creativity and problem-solving. The excitement of building something tangible can overshadow the necessity of thorough planning and requirements analysis. This is especially true when faced with a specific task or problem to solve, leading developers to rush into implementation without fully understanding the broader context.

Consider a scenario where a development team is tasked with creating a new feature for an application.

/* no comments*/

The developers may enthusiastically jump into coding, thinking, **"This will be easy; let's just add this feature as quickly as possible."**
/* still no comments*/

However, this often results in a narrow focus on the immediate solution, neglecting critical aspects such as user experience, scalability, and alignment with business goals.

And what about reliability? Some developers don't even think about preventing or at least helping the software to behave nice when exceptions occur.

Is it the programming language that simply does not offer a try-catch mechanism? Of course, when writing small scripts or basic automation, the developer is entitled to chose if the scripts have to handle exceptions but when this script becomes a team's library, the decision should differ.

Focusing on Sunny-Day Scenarios
When developers concentrate on sunny-day scenarios, they envision how their code will function flawlessly under ideal conditions. This perspective can lead to several issues:

Limited Use-Cases: By only considering optimal conditions, developers may overlook potential edge cases and failure scenarios. This can result in software that performs well under certain conditions but fails to meet user expectations or business requirements when faced with real-world complexities.

Technical Debt: The rush to implement solutions without a comprehensive understanding of requirements can lead to the accumulation of technical debt. Developers might create quick fixes or workarounds that, while functional, introduce inefficiencies and increase the complexity of the codebase. But what is the outcome of patch after patch and quick fix after quick fix? What will this be in short time when a new feature has to be introduced and a significant part of the project has to be refactored?

Misalignment with Stakeholder Needs: Focusing solely on implementation details can lead to software that does not align with the actual needs of stakeholders. Developers may inadvertently build features that do not provide real value or solve the intended problems.

Some teams and projects understand the need of a product owner. The product owner is the one who can indicate what's worth being implemented and what needs to be postponed. The product owner has the sole mission to maximize the value of the product and while implementing fancy features might seem attractive, most of them remain simply costs, as they don't bring any value.

MVP Approach and Time to Market

Introduction
In the world of software development, one of the most persistent challenges is balancing **time to market** with the need for creating a polished, fully functional product. This dilemma often leads developers and product teams to face two competing strategies:

Immediate Implementation (the temptation to build everything at once and launch quickly) and the **Minimum Viable Product (MVP) approach**, which emphasizes launching with just the essential features first and iterating over time.

Each approach has its strengths and weaknesses. The decision of whether to choose immediate implementation or the MVP route often depends on factors like business goals, resource availability, market conditions, and long-term vision. In this chapter, we'll explore the pros and cons of each approach in detail, helping you understand how to navigate the challenges of time-to-market pressure while maintaining a focus on delivering value to your users.

Immediate Implementation: The All-In-One Approach

The **Immediate Implementation** strategy involves developing a full-featured product in one go, with the intent of launching it as a comprehensive solution from day one. Teams that opt for this approach often aim to meet ambitious deadlines or create a product that competes head-to-head with existing market players from the outset.

Pros of Immediate Implementation

Comprehensive User Experience: By building all the features in one go, you can create a cohesive, feature-rich experience from the beginning. Users don't have to wait for future updates or deal with the incomplete nature of a minimum viable product.

Lower Initial User Frustration: With a full feature set available at launch, users are less likely to encounter limitations that may detract from their experience. For example, in contrast to an MVP, which may omit certain critical features, immediate implementation can offer users a complete solution right away.

All-in-One Solution: A feature-rich launch can establish your product as an all-in-one solution, reducing the need for users to rely on third-party tools or competitors' offerings. This could give your product a competitive edge from the get-go.

Clear Market Positioning: Launching with a complete feature set can help a product make a strong initial impression in the market. Customers may view the product as a comprehensive solution, helping to differentiate it from competitors.

Cons of Immediate Implementation

Higher Upfront Costs: Immediate implementation requires significant upfront investment in both time and resources. It involves extensive planning, design, and development, which may be costly for startups or teams with limited budgets.

Increased Risk of Failure: Building a full-featured product without first testing the core concept or its most essential features can be risky. If the product fails to meet market expectations, the team may have wasted substantial resources on features that are ultimately unnecessary or not desired by users.

Longer Time to Market: The more features you build into the product, the longer it takes to get to market. This delay could allow competitors to release their products first, potentially grabbing the attention of your target audience and forcing you to play catch-up.

Inflexibility: Once a product with a full set of features is launched, making changes can be difficult, especially if user feedback indicates the need for significant revisions. Immediate implementation can lock teams into a direction, making it hard to pivot or adapt based on market demands or new insights.

The Minimum Viable Product (MVP) Approach

The **Minimum Viable Product (MVP)** approach, by contrast, focuses on releasing the most basic version of a product — containing only the essential features needed to satisfy early adopters and validate the core concept. The goal is to gather feedback, learn from users, and iterate before investing heavily in additional features.

Pros of the MVP Approach

Faster Time to Market: By focusing on just the core features, the MVP approach allows for faster development and quicker release. This is especially important in competitive markets where being the first to launch can provide a significant advantage.

Cost-Effective: With fewer features and less complexity, building an MVP is often more cost-effective, especially for startups and small teams. It allows businesses to test the waters before committing larger resources to full-scale development.

Early User Feedback: One of the biggest advantages of the MVP approach is the opportunity to gather early feedback from actual users.
This feedback helps refine the product and ensure that you are building something that truly meets market needs. The ability to pivot based on this feedback is invaluable.

Focus on Core Value Proposition: An MVP forces teams to focus on the core value that their product offers. This can help avoid feature bloat and unnecessary complexity, ensuring that the product solves a specific problem effectively.

Cons of the MVP Approach

Limited Features: The MVP approach deliberately omits many features, which can sometimes frustrate users who expect a more polished or comprehensive product. Users may feel that the MVP lacks critical functionality, which could deter them from continuing to use the product.

Potential for Negative Perception: Because MVPs are typically more basic, they can suffer from negative perceptions in the market. If the product isn't well-received due to missing features or bugs, it can create a lasting impression of low quality, even if future iterations improve significantly.

Difficulty in Gaining Traction: Some users may hesitate to adopt a product that feels incomplete or "rough around the edges." This can make it harder to gain traction in a competitive market where users may prefer a more polished, feature-rich experience from the outset.

Challenges in Maintaining Momentum: If the MVP doesn't gain traction quickly, it can be difficult to maintain the momentum required for continued development. Teams might find themselves caught in a cycle of revisiting features without ever truly finding a scalable, successful product-market fit.

Time to Market and Strategy Alignment

The tension between **Immediate Implementation** and **MVP** often boils down to the **time-to-market** challenge. In a world where speed and market timing are critical, an MVP can be an essential strategy for quickly establishing a presence in the market, testing assumptions, and iterating based on user needs. In contrast, immediate implementation is often favored when the product requires a robust feature set to be competitive or meet user expectations.

For startups, an MVP is often the preferred path due to limited resources and the need for early validation. It allows businesses to test hypotheses, reduce risk, and conserve capital. **For established companies**, especially those with significant resources, immediate implementation can be more feasible and appealing, as it allows them to offer a fully formed solution that meets customer expectations from the outset.

Conclusion

Both **Immediate Implementation** and the **MVP approach** offer distinct advantages, and neither strategy is inherently better than the other. The choice between them depends on the specific goals of the project, the resources available, and the competitive landscape. Immediate implementation might be the right choice for teams that need to deliver a comprehensive solution to meet specific business needs or competitive pressures. On the other hand, an MVP approach is a smarter choice for validating ideas, minimizing upfront investment, and iterating based on user feedback.

Ultimately, understanding the trade-offs and aligning the development strategy with business goals is key to delivering a successful product, whether through an MVP or a fully realized solution.

The key to **a successful MVP** release is to present it to customers as it is, as an MVP, with limited functionality, incomplete testing, an optimistic implementation only meant to validate assumptions and obtain fast feedback.

The Importance of Understanding the Big Picture

Identifying Stakeholders

A critical first step in any software development project is identifying and engaging stakeholders. Stakeholders can include end-users, business leaders, and anyone who will be affected by the software solution. By understanding who these individuals are, developers can begin to shape their approach to ensure alignment with organizational goals.

When stakeholders in a software development project are not properly identified, several risks can arise that can significantly impact the project's success, timeline, and overall quality. Proper stakeholder identification is crucial because it ensures that the needs, expectations, and requirements of all parties are addressed, preventing miscommunication and misalignment. Below are some of the key risks associated with not properly identifying stakeholders in software development:

Misaligned Expectations

Failing to identify key stakeholders early in a project can result in their expectations being overlooked during development. This oversight often leads to a product that misses the mark in addressing the true needs or preferences of users, business leaders, or other essential groups. For instance, end-users, marketing teams, or external partners may have distinct priorities or feature requests that, if ignored, could cause dissatisfaction once the product is launched.

Scope Creep

Without clear stakeholder identification, there is a greater likelihood of **scope creep**, where additional features or requirements are added without proper review or approval. This can happen if new stakeholders appear throughout the project or if initial stakeholders were not clear about their needs. Scope creep can lead to delays, increased costs, and a product that is over-engineered or lacks focus.

Source: *Agile Methodology* highlights that regular stakeholder feedback is key to maintaining the project scope and avoiding unnecessary changes during development.

Lack of Clear Requirements

If stakeholders aren't properly identified and engaged, there may be a lack of clarity regarding what the software should achieve. This ambiguity can result in incomplete or conflicting requirements that complicate the development process, leading to wasted time on features that aren't important or missing features that are essential.

Source: *IEEE Software Engineering Standards* stresses the importance of clear communication with all relevant stakeholders to ensure requirements are comprehensive and aligned.

Poor Decision Making

Not having the right stakeholders involved in decision-making can lead to poor decisions that affect the software's quality, usability, and functionality.
Without input from key stakeholders, such as users, business owners, or technical experts, decisions made by the development team may not align with business objectives, user needs, or technological constraints.

Source: *Harvard Business Review* reports that involving the right people in the decision-making process improves the likelihood of making decisions that are beneficial for the project's success.

Delayed Timelines

If stakeholders aren't identified, they may not be engaged in the planning phase or throughout the development process, leading to delays. For example, if approvals or feedback are delayed from critical stakeholders, it can slow down progress and potentially require rework, pushing the project timeline further out.

Source: *Project Management Institute (PMI)* emphasizes that effective stakeholder management can help keep a project on track and within its intended timeline.

User Acceptance Issues

If end-users or other critical stakeholders are not identified or consulted early on, they may reject the final product because it doesn't meet their needs or expectations. Failure to involve the right stakeholders, particularly the end users, often leads to poor user adoption and lower product satisfaction.
Source: *Nielsen Norman Group* has shown that involving users throughout the development process increases the likelihood of creating a product that is both usable and desirable.

Financial and Legal Risks

Inadequate stakeholder identification could also lead to financial or legal risks, especially if regulatory bodies, investors, or key business partners are not properly engaged. For example, if a product is not compliant with relevant laws or standards, it could result in penalties or additional development costs.

Source: *The Software Engineering Institute* discusses how identifying all stakeholders, including legal and compliance officers, helps mitigate the risk of regulatory violations.

Conclusion

Proper stakeholder identification is essential to ensure that software development aligns with business goals, user needs, and regulatory requirements. Failing to identify stakeholders can result in misaligned expectations, scope creep, poor decision-making, and delays, all of which can compromise the success of the project. By engaging stakeholders early and continuously throughout the development lifecycle, teams can reduce risks and deliver a product that meets the needs of its intended audience.

Documenting Requests

Once stakeholders are identified, it is essential to document their requests and expectations thoroughly. This documentation process goes beyond merely capturing requirements; it involves active engagement with stakeholders to clarify their needs. Developers should aim to understand not just what stakeholders think they want, but also the underlying problems they are trying to solve.

Shaping Stakeholder Understanding

Engaging stakeholders in a collaborative manner can help guide them toward a clearer understanding of their needs. Rather than merely capturing requirements, developers can facilitate discussions that lead to insights about what stakeholders truly want. By asking probing questions and exploring potential solutions together, developers can help stakeholders refine their ideas and uncover better solutions.

For example, instead of accepting a request for a specific feature, a developer might ask:
"What problem are you trying to solve with this feature? Can we explore alternative approaches that might achieve your goals more effectively?"
This approach fosters a collaborative atmosphere, encouraging stakeholders to think critically about their needs and consider broader possibilities.

Leading Requirements Elicitation Instead of Capturing

The Shift in Mindset
Transitioning from requirements capturing to requirements elicitation requires a fundamental shift in mindset. Developers must see themselves not merely as implementers of predefined specifications but as partners in the solution-building process. This shift necessitates a deeper understanding of both the business context and user needs.

Collaborative Workshops and Prototyping
One effective method for leading requirements elicitation is through collaborative workshops.

These sessions bring together stakeholders and developers to brainstorm and discuss potential solutions. Utilizing techniques such as story mapping or prototyping can help visualize ideas and encourage active participation.

For instance, a developer might present a rough prototype of a feature during a workshop, allowing stakeholders to provide immediate feedback. This iterative process can lead to more informed decisions and a better understanding of what the final product should look like.

Prioritization of Requirements

Once a clearer understanding of stakeholder needs is established, it becomes essential to prioritize requirements. Developers can work with stakeholders to determine which features provide the most value and align with strategic objectives. This prioritization process ensures that the development team focuses on delivering the most impactful solutions first, avoiding the trap of feature bloat.

Avoiding the Pitfalls of

Detail-Driven Development

Balancing Detail with Vision

While attention to detail is undoubtedly important in software development, it must be balanced with a focus on the overarching vision. Developers should regularly step back and assess whether their work aligns with the project's goals. Engaging in periodic reviews and reflections can help maintain this balance.

Emphasizing Documentation and Communication

Thorough documentation and open communication channels are vital for ensuring that everyone involved in the project remains aligned. Developers should maintain clear records of stakeholder interactions, requirements discussions, and design decisions. This documentation serves as a reference point throughout the development process and helps mitigate misunderstandings.

Iterative Development Practices

Adopting iterative development practices, such as Agile methodologies, can help developers maintain focus on the big picture while allowing for detailed implementation work. Regular sprint reviews and retrospectives encourage continuous improvement and keep the team aligned with stakeholder expectations.

Conclusion

The temptation to jump straight into coding often leads to a narrow focus on partial sunny-day scenarios. This approach can result in the creation of automation for limited use cases, ultimately failing to build the right thing. By emphasizing the importance of identifying stakeholders, documenting their requests, and engaging in requirements elicitation, developers can better understand the true needs of the business and end-users.

Shifting from a mindset of requirements capturing to one of leading requirements elicitation encourages collaboration and fosters a clearer understanding of project goals. By guiding stakeholders toward a more comprehensive vision, developers can propose innovative solutions that deliver real value. Ultimately, balancing attention to detail with an awareness of the big picture is essential for successful software development, ensuring that teams build not just for today's sunny-day scenarios, but for the diverse realities of the future.

How to build it right?

Designing Software Architecture with Qualities in Mind: A Guide to Building the Right Foundation

In the world of software development, building the right architecture is crucial for creating systems that not only meet current requirements but also adapt to future needs. Software architects play a pivotal role in this process, guiding the design and implementation of systems that prioritize essential architecture qualities. This article provides a comprehensive overview of how to begin designing a proper architecture with qualities in mind, introducing the architecture qualities outlined by the arc42 framework, such as extensibility, debuggability, scalability, and more.

The Importance of Software Architecture

Understanding Software Architecture
Software architecture serves as the blueprint for a system, outlining its structure, components, and interactions. A well-defined architecture provides a framework for decision-making throughout the software development lifecycle, ensuring that all stakeholders share a common understanding of the system's goals and constraints.

The Role of Architecture Qualities

Architecture qualities represent the non-functional requirements that significantly impact a system's success.

These qualities guide the architectural design process and help ensure that the resulting system can meet its performance, maintainability, and usability goals. Prioritizing these qualities early in the design process lays the groundwork for a robust and adaptable system.

A risk often ignored

While architecture decisions and priorities seem clear and unquestionable sometimes, later developers and the product team, when trying to add other features or dependencies, faces the cost of undocumented architecture decisions, that are not only hard to understand, but might even block the implementation of some features without significant rework.

Starting the Architecture Design Process

Defining Stakeholder Goals and Constraints

Before diving into architectural design, it is essential to engage stakeholders to understand their goals and constraints. This involves:

Conducting Stakeholder Interviews: Gathering insights from business leaders, end-users, and other key stakeholders to identify their expectations and concerns.

Creating User Personas: Developing profiles of typical users to better understand their needs and the context in which they will use the system.

Documenting Business Goals: Clearly outlining the business objectives that the system must support, such as increasing revenue, improving user satisfaction, or reducing operational costs.

Establishing Quality Attribute Goals

Once stakeholder goals are established, the next step is to identify and prioritize the architecture qualities that are most relevant to the project. Some key qualities to consider include:

Extensibility: The ease with which the system can be extended to accommodate new features or changes in requirements. This quality ensures that the architecture can adapt as the business evolves.

Debuggability: The ability to diagnose and fix issues within the system efficiently. A design that prioritizes debuggability facilitates troubleshooting and maintenance, ultimately improving system reliability.

Scalability: The capacity of the system to handle increased workloads or user demands. Scalability is critical for ensuring that the system can grow alongside the business without requiring a complete redesign.

Performance: The system's ability to meet response time and throughput requirements under various conditions. Performance considerations must be integrated into the architecture from the outset.

Security: Ensuring that the architecture incorporates security measures to protect sensitive data and maintain user trust. Security should be treated as a core aspect of the design rather than an afterthought.

Analyzing Trade-offs and Making Informed Decisions

Architectural design often involves making trade-offs between competing qualities. For example, a system designed for maximum extensibility might face challenges in achieving optimal performance. To navigate these trade-offs:

Use Quality Attribute Scenarios: These scenarios help architects understand how different qualities will be impacted under various conditions. By exploring "what if" scenarios, architects can assess the implications of design choices and make informed decisions.

Collaborate with Stakeholders: Engaging stakeholders in discussions about trade-offs can provide valuable perspectives. This collaboration ensures that decisions align with overall business goals.

Key Architectural Principles

Separation of Concerns
One of the foundational principles of software architecture is the separation of concerns. By dividing the system into distinct components or layers, each responsible for a specific aspect of functionality, architects can enhance modularity and maintainability. This principle facilitates independent development and testing, making it easier to implement changes without affecting other parts of the system.

Encapsulation
Encapsulation involves hiding the internal workings of a component from the rest of the system, exposing only the necessary interfaces. This principle promotes loose coupling between components, reducing dependencies and enhancing the system's flexibility. Changes made within one component are less likely to impact others, improving overall stability.

Use of Design Patterns
Design patterns provide proven solutions to common architectural problems. Familiarity with design patterns allows architects to leverage best practices and avoid reinventing the wheel. Some commonly used design patterns in software architecture include:

Microservices Architecture: Emphasizes the development of small, independently deployable services that can communicate through APIs, promoting scalability and extensibility.

Layered Architecture: Organizes the system into layers, each responsible for specific functionality (e.g., presentation, business logic, data access), facilitating separation of concerns.

Event-Driven Architecture: Uses events to trigger interactions between components, promoting loose coupling and scalability.

Plugin architecture in software is a design pattern that allows an application to extend its functionality dynamically by adding modular components, known as plugins. These plugins are independent units that integrate seamlessly with the core application through predefined interfaces or APIs. This architecture provides flexibility, enabling developers or third-party contributors to enhance or customize the software without modifying its core codebase. Common in software like web browsers, IDEs, and media players, plugin architectures promote scalability and adaptability while adhering to principles like separation of concerns and modularity.

Documenting the Architecture

Creating Architectural Diagrams

Visual representations of the architecture are invaluable for communicating design decisions to stakeholders. Architects should create diagrams that illustrate key components, their interactions, and the overall structure of the system. Common types of architectural diagrams include:

Component Diagrams: Show how different components of the system interact with each other.

Sequence Diagrams: Detail the flow of messages between components over time.

Deployment Diagrams: Illustrate how components are deployed in the environment, including hardware and network configurations.

Maintaining Comprehensive Documentation

In addition to diagrams, thorough documentation is essential for ensuring that the architectural design is well understood and can be maintained over time. Architects should document:

Architectural Decisions: Record the rationale behind key design choices, including trade-offs made during the decision-making process.

Quality Attribute Goals: Clearly define the architecture qualities that the system aims to achieve, along with the corresponding metrics for evaluation.

Implementation Guidelines: Provide guidance for developers on how to implement features in alignment with the architectural vision.

What Is the Right Level of Architecture Documentation in Software?

The right level of architecture documentation is a balancing act between clarity and efficiency. Too much documentation risks overwhelming developers with unnecessary details, while too little can leave teams navigating ambiguity.

An effective documentation strategy should align with the project's complexity, team size, and long-term maintenance goals.
Architecture documentation serves as a blueprint, guiding stakeholders on key decisions about structure, dependencies, and interactions within the system.

For small or agile teams, lightweight documentation like diagrams or concise decision records often suffices. Agile emphasizes "just enough documentation," meaning teams document only what is needed to clarify critical architecture decisions or onboard new members.

Tools such as Architecture Decision Records (ADRs) provide a streamlined way to capture design choices without excessive overhead. However, for larger teams or enterprise-level projects, more comprehensive documentation, such as component diagrams, API specs, and non-functional requirement definitions, becomes essential to maintain alignment.

One vital consideration is the evolving nature of software. Architecture documentation should be a living artifact that evolves with the codebase. Static documents can quickly become outdated, leading to potential miscommunication or technical debt.

Version-controlled documentation repositories, supported by tools like Markdown, PlantUML, or Confluence, enable teams to maintain up-to-date and accessible records. Integrating documentation updates into development workflows ensures it reflects the system's current state without becoming a burden.

Ultimately, the right level of documentation depends on your team and system's unique needs. High-level diagrams may suffice for early stages or small projects, while more granular details are crucial for compliance-heavy or mission-critical applications.
By tailoring the documentation to fit the audience and context, teams can foster collaboration and understanding while avoiding the inefficiencies of over-documentation or the risks of under-documentation.

Conclusion

Designing a proper software architecture with qualities in mind is a critical step toward building systems that are robust, maintainable, and adaptable to future needs. By starting with a clear understanding of stakeholder goals, prioritizing architecture qualities, and employing key architectural principles, architects can lay a strong foundation for successful software development.

Incorporating the architecture qualities outlined by the arc42 framework, such as extensibility, debuggability, scalability, and others, ensures that the resulting system aligns with both business objectives and user expectations. As the architecture design process unfolds, architects must remain vigilant about documenting their decisions and fostering collaboration with stakeholders to create a shared understanding of the system's vision.

As we delve deeper into architecture qualities in the next chapter, we will explore specific strategies for achieving these qualities and the metrics for evaluating success. By prioritizing architecture qualities from the outset, architects can significantly enhance the likelihood of delivering a software solution that not only meets immediate requirements but also positions the organization for long-term success.

Questions for software architects

The Importance of Documenting Architecture Decisions: A Guide for Software Architects

"Where are your architecture decisions documented?"

This seemingly simple question can reveal a great deal about the health and longevity of a software project. Documenting architectural decisions is a critical yet often overlooked aspect of software development. Failing to adequately document these decisions can lead to confusion, misalignment, and technical debt, ultimately jeopardizing the success of the project. In this article, we will explore why documenting architecture decisions is important, how to do it effectively, and when to engage in this essential practice.

What Coud Happen If Decisions Are Not Documented?

Loss of Knowledge

One of the most significant risks of failing to document architectural decisions is the loss of knowledge. In any software project, team members may come and go, and as people leave, their understanding of the architecture often departs with them. Without documentation, new team members face a steep learning curve, and existing members may struggle to remember the rationale behind certain choices.

This knowledge gap can lead to misunderstandings and inconsistencies in the implementation of features.

Not documenting software architecture decisions can lead to significant issues in understanding and maintaining the system. Without clear documentation, developers and team members may struggle to grasp why certain design choices were made, leading to inconsistent implementation or confusion during future development. New team members may face difficulties in getting up to speed, and important architectural context may be lost over time, hindering collaboration. This lack of clarity can also increase the likelihood of redundant or conflicting solutions being introduced, as teams may unknowingly reinvent or contradict previous decisions.

Another risk is the potential for poor decision-making when facing changes or updates to the system. Without documented decisions, it becomes much harder to assess the impact of modifying key architectural components. Teams may overlook critical dependencies or interactions between system parts, leading to unforeseen consequences that compromise the system's stability, performance, or scalability. In the absence of clear architectural guidance, teams may opt for quick fixes that seem expedient but create long-term technical debt, further complicating future enhancements or troubleshooting.

Finally, not documenting architecture decisions can pose a serious risk in terms of compliance, auditing, and knowledge transfer. For projects subject to regulatory or industry standards, a lack of documentation can prevent the organization from demonstrating adherence to required practices. Furthermore, as staff turnover occurs, the absence of detailed records can result in the loss of valuable knowledge, making it difficult to retain institutional expertise. This can leave organizations vulnerable to errors, inefficiencies, and missed opportunities for improvement, as future developers will lack a comprehensive understanding of the architecture's design and rationale.

Increased Technical Debt

When architectural decisions are not documented, it becomes challenging to assess the long-term impact of those decisions. Teams may inadvertently introduce changes that conflict with the architecture's original intent, leading to increased technical debt. This accumulated debt can hinder the development process, making it more difficult to introduce new features or adapt the system to changing requirements.

Difficulty in Maintaining Alignment

Architectural decisions are often made in response to stakeholder requirements, technical constraints, or strategic goals. When these decisions are not documented, the alignment between the architecture and the broader business objectives can deteriorate. Teams may lose sight of the reasons behind specific design choices, leading to decisions that stray from the intended direction of the project.

Inefficient Communication

Effective communication is essential in any development team. Without documentation of architectural decisions, team members may find it challenging to discuss and understand the rationale behind certain design choices. This can lead to debates, confusion, and delays in the development process. Clear documentation serves as a reference point for discussions, helping teams to communicate more effectively.

Why Is Documenting Architecture Decisions Important?

Preserving Institutional Knowledge

Documenting architecture decisions helps preserve institutional knowledge within the team. By recording the reasons behind each decision, teams can ensure that future members have access to the context and rationale necessary to understand the architecture. This is especially crucial in long-term projects where team turnover may be high.

Supporting Decision-Making

Architecture documentation provides a valuable resource for decision-making. When teams face new challenges or changes in requirements, they can refer to past decisions to inform their next steps. This historical context can help prevent the repetition of mistakes and facilitate more informed choices.

Enhancing Collaboration

Documentation encourages collaboration by providing a shared understanding of the architecture. When all team members can access and review the same documentation, it fosters a culture of openness and transparency. This collaborative environment enables team members to contribute to architectural discussions and helps align everyone on the project's goals.

Facilitating Change Management

As systems evolve, architectural changes are often necessary. Comprehensive documentation makes it easier to assess the impact of proposed changes on the overall architecture.

By understanding the original decisions and their implications, teams can make more informed choices about how to proceed, minimizing disruption and ensuring that changes align with project goals.

How to Document Architecture Decisions

Choose the Right Format

The format of documentation can vary based on the team's needs and preferences. Some common formats for documenting architectural decisions include:

Decision Records: Simple templates that capture key details of each decision, including the context, options considered, the chosen solution, and the rationale.

Architecture Diagrams: Visual representations of the system architecture that can complement written documentation and provide clarity on the relationships between components.

Wiki or Knowledge Base: A centralized platform where all architectural documentation can be stored and easily accessed by team members.

Choosing the right format depends on the complexity of the architecture and the preferences of the team.

Capture Key Information

When documenting architectural decisions, it's essential to capture key information that provides context and clarity. Each entry should include:

Decision Title: A brief and descriptive title summarizing the decision.

Date: The date when the decision was made.

Context: A description of the circumstances that led to the decision, including any relevant stakeholder input or technical constraints.

Options Considered: A summary of the alternatives that were evaluated, including their pros and cons.

Chosen Solution: A clear statement of the decision made, along with any relevant technical details.

Rationale: An explanation of why the chosen solution was preferred over other options.

Consequences: Any potential impacts or trade-offs associated with the decision, including future considerations or follow-up actions.

Engage the Team in Documentation

Encouraging team members to contribute to documentation fosters a sense of ownership and collaboration. Architects and lead developers should establish a culture where documenting decisions is viewed as a shared responsibility. Regularly scheduled retrospectives or review sessions can provide opportunities for the team to reflect on recent decisions and ensure that they are appropriately documented.

Maintain and Update Documentation

Documentation should not be a one-time effort. As projects evolve, architectural decisions may need to be revisited, updated, or expanded. Establishing a process for reviewing and maintaining documentation ensures that it remains relevant and accurate. This can include periodic audits of existing documentation, especially after significant architectural changes or project milestones.

When to Document Architecture Decisions

During the Design Phase

The most critical time to document architectural decisions is during the design phase of a project. As architects evaluate options and make decisions, capturing this information in real time helps ensure that the documentation accurately reflects the context and rationale behind each choice.

When Changes Occur

Any time a significant change is made to the architecture, whether due to new requirements, technical challenges, or shifts in business strategy, it is crucial to update the documentation accordingly.

Changes can introduce new complexities or invalidate previous decisions, making it essential to capture this information promptly.

In Retrospectives and Review Meetings

Regular retrospectives and review meetings provide excellent opportunities to revisit architectural decisions.

Teams should use these sessions to reflect on recent decisions, assess their outcomes, and update documentation as necessary. This practice ensures that documentation remains a living resource that evolves alongside the project.

Conclusion

Documenting architecture decisions is a vital practice that can significantly impact the success and sustainability of a software project. By preserving institutional knowledge, supporting decision-making, enhancing collaboration, and facilitating change management, comprehensive documentation helps teams navigate the complexities of software architecture.

Neglecting to document architectural decisions can lead to confusion, increased technical debt, and misalignment with stakeholder goals. By prioritizing documentation throughout the design process and establishing a culture of collaboration and transparency, software architects can lay a strong foundation for their projects. As teams continue to evolve, the documentation of architectural decisions will serve as a valuable resource, guiding future development efforts and ensuring that the architecture remains aligned with business objectives.

As we move forward in our exploration of software architecture, we will delve deeper into specific strategies for documenting architectural qualities and decision-making processes, empowering teams to create systems that are robust, adaptable, and successful.

Designing Software Architectures for People: Bridging Communication Through Effective Documentation

"Code is read much more often than it is written," a sentiment famously expressed by *Phil Karlton*, emphasizes the importance of readability in software development. This principle extends beyond code; it is equally applicable to software architecture.

Just as code should be clear and understandable to developers, architecture documentation must be accessible and interpretable by a diverse range of audiences, including stakeholders, designers, and developers.

In this article, we will explore how to create architecture that prioritizes readability, discuss the role of various documentation systems like UML, introduce C4 diagrams as a communication tool, and advocate for the "Documentation as Code" approach, emphasizing the use of markdown languages such as AsciiDoc or Markdown.

The Importance of Readable Architecture Documentation

Architecture for People

Software architecture is fundamentally about making decisions that affect not only the technical aspects of a system but also the people who will interact with it.

A well-documented architecture facilitates effective communication among all stakeholders, ensuring that everyone has a shared understanding of the system's goals and constraints. When architectures are made for people to read, they foster collaboration and alignment within the team.

Readable documentation helps bridge the gap between technical and non-technical audiences, enabling stakeholders to engage meaningfully in discussions about the architecture and its implications for the business.

The Limitations of UML

Unified Modeling Language (UML) has long been a standard for visualizing software architecture. However, its complexity can sometimes hinder effective communication.

While UML provides a rich set of symbols and diagrams, not everyone in the audience may be familiar with them. This can lead to misunderstandings and misinterpretations of the architecture.

Using UML as the sole method of documenting architecture can inadvertently exclude non-technical stakeholders who may struggle to grasp the intricacies of UML diagrams. Consequently, the goal of conveying architectural decisions effectively can be undermined.

Transmitting the Message to All Audiences

The true essence of architecture documentation lies not in adherence to specific systems like UML but in the ability to transmit messages to all kinds of audiences. The focus should be on clarity, accessibility, and relevance. This is where the concept of C4 diagrams shines.

C4 Diagrams: A Framework for Communication

What Are C4 Diagrams?

C4 (Context, Containers, Components, and Code) diagrams provide a visual framework for representing software architecture at various levels of abstraction.

Developed by *Simon Brown*, this approach emphasizes simplicity and clarity while addressing different audiences' needs.

Context Diagram: Provides a high-level view of the system, showing how it interacts with external entities, such as users and other systems.

Container Diagram: Breaks down the system into containers (applications or services) and shows how they interact.

Component Diagram: Focuses on the internal structure of a container, detailing the components that make it up and their interactions.

Code Diagram: Illustrates the implementation details of individual components, suitable for developers.

Whom Do C4 Diagrams Help?

C4 diagrams cater to a broad audience, making them ideal for various stakeholders:

Business Stakeholders: The context diagram provides a simple overview of the system's relationships, helping business stakeholders understand its relevance to the organization.

Developers and Architects: Container and component diagrams deliver the necessary technical details for developers and architects, enabling them to understand how the system is structured and how to contribute effectively.

QA and Operations Teams: Clear documentation helps QA and operations teams grasp the architecture, which is vital for testing and deployment processes.

How to Create C4 Diagrams Properly
To effectively create C4 diagrams:
Keep It Simple: Avoid clutter and focus on the essential elements. The goal is to convey information clearly and concisely.

Use Clear Labels: Ensure that all components, containers, and relationships are labeled accurately to enhance understanding.

Iterate Based on Feedback: Share drafts with team members to gather feedback and make necessary adjustments. This collaborative approach enhances the overall quality of the diagrams.

Making Architecture Documentation

Presentable

Visual Design for Clarity
To ensure that architecture documentation is not only informative but also visually appealing, it is crucial to consider its presentation.

```
/* it might look good on a display */
/* how does it look in a projector */
/* with limited resolution and limited colors? */
```

When displayed on a projector or large screen, clarity and readability should be prioritized. Here are several guidelines to enhance the presentation of architectural diagrams and documents:

Use Meaningful Visuals: Entities in diagrams should represent concrete concepts, such as actors, humans, and servers, rather than abstract squares and rectangles. This approach helps audiences quickly grasp the roles and relationships within the architecture.

Font and Colors: Choose fonts that are legible from a distance and maintain a professional appearance. Use contrasting colors to differentiate between various elements (e.g., actors, systems, components) while ensuring that the overall design is visually coherent. This aids in guiding the audience's attention and enhancing comprehension.

Consistent Layout: Maintain a consistent layout throughout the documentation to create a familiar structure. Use headers, bullet points, and spacing to break up text, making it easier to follow along during presentations.

Accessibility Considerations: Ensure that color choices are accessible to individuals with color vision deficiencies. Avoid relying solely on color to convey information; instead, consider using labels, patterns, or textures for differentiation.

The Role of Presentations

When presenting architectural documentation, it's essential to engage the audience. Utilize storytelling techniques to explain how the architecture aligns with business goals and user needs. By doing so, architects can transform technical documentation into a narrative that resonates with all stakeholders.

Documenting Architecture Using Text and Markdown

Text Documentation: A Foundation for Clarity
While diagrams are essential for visualizing architecture, textual documentation remains crucial for conveying detailed information. Text documentation allows for deeper explanations, rationale, and context surrounding architectural decisions.

Markdown and AsciiDoc: Modern Documentation Formats
Using markup languages like **Markdown** and **AsciiDoc** streamlines the documentation process. These languages offer several advantages:

Simplicity: They are easy to learn and use, allowing developers to focus on content rather than formatting.

Readability: Documentation written in Markdown or AsciiDoc is inherently more readable in plain text form, making it accessible to a wider audience.

Compatibility: Both formats can be converted into various output formats (HTML, PDF, etc.), making it easier to share and distribute documentation.

Documentation as Code

The "Documentation as Code" movement aligns with the broader trend of "Everything as Code," emphasizing that documentation should be treated with the same importance as code itself. This approach has several benefits:

Version Control: Just like code, documentation can be version-controlled using Git, enabling teams to track changes, collaborate, and roll back if needed.

Consistency: Using the same tools and processes for documentation as for code helps maintain consistency and quality across the board.

Automated Generation: With structured documentation practices, teams can automate the generation of documentation from code comments, reducing the manual effort required to keep documentation up to date.

Structured Reuse of Concepts and Definitions

Leveraging Tools Like Structurizer
To facilitate the structured reuse of architectural concepts and definitions, tools like **Structurizer [https://structurizr.com]** can be employed. These tools allow teams to create a repository of architectural elements, enabling consistent use across different projects. But while it facilitates creating the documentation, does it facilitate reading it or presenting it on a projector or smart white board? Yes, the entities are there but how is the readability considering fonts and colors?

Creating a Knowledge Base

Building a centralized knowledge base for architectural decisions, patterns, and guidelines empowers teams to reference established practices and reduce redundancy. This repository can include:

Design Patterns: Documenting common design patterns used within the architecture.

Architectural Principles: Outlining guiding principles that shape design decisions.

Lessons Learned: Capturing insights from past projects to inform future architectural endeavors.

Conclusion

Creating architecture that is made for people to read is essential for successful software development. By focusing on clarity and accessibility rather than rigid adherence to specific systems like UML, architects can ensure effective communication among diverse audiences. C4 diagrams serve as a valuable tool for bridging the gap between technical and non-technical stakeholders, facilitating a shared understanding of architectural decisions.

Moreover, embracing documentation as code and utilizing modern markup languages like Markdown and AsciiDoc can enhance the quality and maintainability of architecture documentation. By treating documentation with the same level of care as code, teams can create a robust knowledge base that supports collaboration and informs future development efforts.

Finally, by making architecture documentation visually appealing and engaging, teams can foster deeper understanding and alignment among stakeholders. As the software landscape continues to evolve, prioritizing clear and effective architecture documentation will be crucial for enabling organizations to build resilient and adaptable systems that meet the needs of their stakeholders.

The Evolution of Architecture Documentation: Generated from Code vs. Manually Created Diagrams

As software systems grow in complexity, the need for effective architecture documentation becomes increasingly critical. Traditionally, architecture documentation has been manually crafted by architects using specialized tools and designed diagrams. However, recent advancements in technology have led to the emergence of tools that can generate architecture documentation directly from code. This article explores the pros and cons of both approaches, aiming to provide insight into how organizations can best document their software architecture.

Understanding Architecture Documentation

Architecture documentation serves as a blueprint for a software system, outlining its components, relationships, and interactions. It is crucial for conveying the rationale behind design decisions, guiding future development, and ensuring that all stakeholders have a clear understanding of the system.

There are two primary approaches to architecture documentation:

Manual Documentation: This involves human authors creating documents using tools like Microsoft Visio, Lucidchart, or UML-specific software to illustrate the architecture through diagrams and written descriptions.

Code-Generated Documentation: This approach utilizes tools that extract architectural information directly from the codebase, producing diagrams and documentation automatically.
Both methods have their advantages and disadvantages, which will be examined in detail.

Manual Documentation: The Traditional Approach

Pros
Customization: Manual documentation allows architects to tailor the content and style according to the audience's needs. This flexibility enables them to emphasize specific aspects of the architecture, include narrative explanations, and provide context that automated tools may overlook.

Contextual Clarity: Architects can provide rich context and rationale behind architectural decisions. This includes detailing the trade-offs considered and how different elements align with business goals.

Creative Presentation: With manual documentation, architects can use creative techniques to enhance clarity, such as storytelling, visuals, and analogies. This can make complex concepts more digestible for non-technical stakeholders.

Control Over Quality: Authors can thoroughly review and edit the documentation, ensuring high quality and coherence in messaging. This can prevent misunderstandings that might arise from auto generated content.

Cons

Time-Consuming: Creating manual documentation is often a labor-intensive process. Architects must spend significant time crafting diagrams and writing content, which can detract from their focus on actual development work.

Prone to Obsolescence: Manual documentation can quickly become outdated, especially in agile environments, where code changes frequently. Without regular updates, documentation may fail to reflect the current state of the architecture.

Subjectivity: The quality of manual documentation can vary significantly between authors. Different individuals may have different styles and approaches, leading to inconsistencies in terminology and presentation.

Scalability Challenges: As the codebase and team grow, maintaining comprehensive and up-to-date documentation can become increasingly challenging. This often leads to documentation that is either incomplete or poorly maintained.

Code-Generated Documentation: The Automated Approach

Pros

Efficiency: Code-generated documentation can be produced quickly and automatically, saving architects significant time. As changes are made to the codebase, documentation can be updated almost instantaneously.

Consistency: Automated tools ensure that documentation adheres to predefined standards, promoting uniformity in terminology and style. This is particularly beneficial for large teams with multiple contributors.

Real-time Accuracy: Because the documentation is generated from the code itself, it is always in sync with the latest version. This eliminates the risk of outdated information and ensures that all stakeholders have access to the most current architecture details.

Scalability: Code-generated documentation can easily scale alongside the project. As new components are added, documentation is automatically updated, making it easier to manage complex systems.

Cons

Lack of Context: Automated documentation often lacks the depth of explanation that manual documentation can provide. While it may show relationships and dependencies, it typically does not include the rationale behind design decisions or trade-offs.

Limited Customization: While some tools allow for customization, code-generated documentation is generally constrained by the capabilities of the tools being used. This can limit the ability to tailor content to specific audiences.

Abstract Representation: Generated diagrams may be overly technical or abstract, making it difficult for non-technical stakeholders to grasp the overall architecture. This can hinder effective communication and understanding.

Dependence on Tool Quality: The effectiveness of code-generated documentation is heavily reliant on the quality of the tool used. If the tool fails to accurately interpret the architecture or produces unclear diagrams, the documentation may be less useful.

Choosing the Right Approach:

Balancing the Two Methods

The choice between manual and code-generated documentation is not always a straightforward one. Each method has its unique advantages and challenges, and the most effective approach may often involve a combination of both.

Hybrid Approaches

Code as a Source of Truth: Many organizations adopt a hybrid approach, where code serves as the primary source of architectural truth. Code-generated documentation is maintained to ensure real-time accuracy, while manual documentation is used to provide context and explanations.

Periodic Reviews: Teams can schedule periodic reviews of manually created documents to align them with the codebase. This ensures that the narrative remains relevant while leveraging the efficiency of automated tools.

Selective Manual Documentation: In cases where certain components of the architecture require deeper explanation or narrative context, architects can selectively create manual documentation for those elements while relying on autogenerated content for others.

Utilizing Tools for Diagramming: Architects can use code generation tools to produce base diagrams and then enhance them manually with additional context, annotations, and visual improvements to create more engaging presentations.

Conclusion

Effective architecture documentation is critical for fostering understanding and collaboration among diverse stakeholders in the ever-evolving landscape of software development. Both manual and code-generated documentation approaches offer distinct advantages and disadvantages.

Manual documentation provides customization, contextual clarity, and creative presentation but can be time-consuming and prone to obsolescence. Conversely, code-generated documentation offers efficiency, consistency, and real-time accuracy but may lack context and customization.

Ultimately, organizations should consider adopting a hybrid approach that leverages the strengths of both methods. By combining the immediacy and scalability of code-generated documentation with the richness of manual documentation, teams can create comprehensive architecture documentation that serves the needs of all stakeholders, fostering better communication and alignment throughout the software development lifecycle.

The Risks of Premature Estimation in Software Projects

In the dynamic world of software development, the pressure to deliver quickly often leads teams to jump straight into project estimation. Project managers and stakeholders frequently push for timelines and cost assessments without taking the necessary time to gather and analyze requirements thoroughly. This rush can have significant consequences, jeopardizing the project's success and increasing the likelihood of failure. This chapter delves into the risks associated with premature estimation, emphasizing the importance of initial assessments and proper requirement definitions.

The Impetus for Quick Estimates

External Pressures
The demand for rapid results often stems from external pressures, including market competition, budget constraints, and stakeholder expectations.

When project managers or customers are eager to see progress, they may prioritize swift estimations over a thorough understanding of the requirements. This urgency can lead to a variety of pitfalls, including:

Misalignment of Expectations: Quick estimates can create a false sense of certainty, leading stakeholders to assume that the project is more straightforward than it truly is. This misalignment can cause significant friction between developers and stakeholders as the project unfolds.

Inaccurate Budgeting and Resource Allocation: Without a proper understanding of the project scope, initial cost and resource estimates are often based on assumptions rather than facts.

This can lead to underfunding, insufficient staffing, and a lack of necessary resources, ultimately hindering project progress.

Ignoring Complexity
Jumping to estimates without proper assessment often means ignoring the inherent complexity of software projects. Software systems are rarely linear or simple; they involve intricate interactions among various components, stakeholders, and technologies. As a result, premature estimation can overlook critical factors such as:

Technical Challenges: Estimating without understanding the technical landscape may result in underestimating the challenges posed by legacy systems, integration needs, and new technologies. This can lead to significant roadblocks later in the project.

User Needs: Failing to engage users and stakeholders in the requirement-gathering process can result in misunderstandings about what the software must achieve. This lack of clarity can lead to a product that does not meet user expectations or business objectives.

Consequences of Premature Estimation

Scope Creep
One of the most significant risks of premature estimation is the potential for scope creep. When initial estimates are based on incomplete or inaccurate requirements, the project is likely to evolve in unpredictable ways. As stakeholders recognize that their needs are not being met, they may request additional features or changes, leading to a constantly shifting project scope.

Impact on Timelines: As the project scope expands, timelines can stretch, and the team may struggle to accommodate new requests within the original schedule. This can lead to frustration for both developers and stakeholders.

Increased Costs: Scope creep often results in increased costs as additional resources are required to implement new features or address issues arising from incomplete initial requirements.

Decreased Quality
Rushing into estimates can compromise the quality of the software being developed. When teams feel pressured to meet unrealistic timelines, they may cut corners or skip essential steps in the development process, leading to:

Inadequate Testing: Limited time for testing means that potential defects and issues may go unnoticed until after the software is deployed, leading to a poor user experience and potentially costly fixes.

Technical Debt: Teams may choose quick fixes over long-term solutions, accumulating technical debt that will require additional time and resources to address later. This can hinder the software's maintainability and scalability.

Team Morale and Engagement
The pressure to deliver quickly can also affect team morale. Developers and other team members may feel stressed and overwhelmed when asked to provide estimates without sufficient context. This can lead to:

Burnout: Constantly working under pressure without a clear understanding of project requirements can lead to burnout, affecting team productivity and job satisfaction.

Reduced Collaboration: A focus on rapid estimations may discourage open communication and collaboration among team members. Developers may become reluctant to voice concerns about unrealistic timelines, leading to further misunderstandings.

The Importance of Proper Requirement Assessment

Engaging Stakeholders
To mitigate the risks associated with premature estimation, it is essential to engage stakeholders early in the project. This includes:

Conducting Workshops: Collaborative workshops can help gather requirements, clarify expectations, and ensure all stakeholders have a voice in the process.

Utilizing Techniques: Techniques such as user stories, interviews, and surveys can provide valuable insights into user needs and business objectives, informing more accurate estimates.

Creating a Clear Requirements Document
A well-defined requirements document serves as the foundation for successful project estimation. This document should include:

Functional Requirements: Clear definitions of what the software must do, including user interactions and system behaviors.

Non-Functional Requirements: Criteria such as performance, security, and scalability that the system must meet.

Acceptance Criteria: Clearly defined metrics for how success will be measured, helping to align stakeholder expectations with project outcomes.

Conclusion

The pressure to deliver rapid estimates in software projects can lead to significant risks, including misaligned expectations, scope creep, decreased quality, and negative impacts on team morale. To mitigate these risks, it is crucial to prioritize proper requirement assessments before jumping into estimation.

By engaging stakeholders, conducting thorough workshops, and creating clear requirements documentation, teams can develop more accurate estimates that reflect the project's true complexity. This approach not only helps avoid pitfalls but also fosters better collaboration, increases stakeholder satisfaction, and ultimately leads to the successful delivery of software that meets the needs of its users. In an era where agility and responsiveness are paramount, taking the time to assess requirements upfront can yield substantial long-term benefits for software projects.

Architecture qualities

The Importance of Engaging Stakeholders and Technical Leads in Determining Architecture Qualities

In software development, architecture serves as the foundation upon which systems are built. The architectural decisions made at the outset have long-lasting implications for system performance, maintainability, scalability, and user experience. Given the critical nature of these decisions, it is vital to engage both stakeholders and technical leads in discussions about the architecture qualities that will guide the development process. This article explores why this engagement is crucial and how it can lead to better architectural outcomes.

Understanding Architecture Qualities

Architecture qualities refer to the non-functional requirements that define how a system performs its intended functions. Common architecture qualities include:

Scalability: The ability of the system to handle increased loads or accommodate growth.

Performance: How quickly the system responds to user actions or processes data.

Maintainability: The ease with which the system can be updated or modified.

Security: The measures taken to protect the system from unauthorized access or attacks.

Usability: The ease with which end-users can interact with the system.

These qualities are often interdependent; for example, enhancing security may impact performance, while improving maintainability can affect scalability. Therefore, it is essential to have a clear understanding of which qualities are most critical for the specific project context.

Engaging Stakeholders: Aligning Vision and Goals

Understanding Business Objectives

Stakeholders, including business leaders, product owners, and end-users, have unique perspectives that can significantly influence architectural decisions.

Engaging these stakeholders ensures that the architecture aligns with the overall business objectives. For example:

Prioritizing Features: Stakeholders can provide insights into which features are most valuable to users, helping architects prioritize qualities such as performance and usability.

Long-term Vision: Understanding the strategic goals of the organization allows architects to design systems that support future growth and change, such as scalability and flexibility.

Identifying Pain Points

Stakeholders often have firsthand experience with existing systems and can highlight pain points that must be addressed in the new architecture. These insights are invaluable for identifying:

User Experience Issues: End-users can share their experiences, helping architects prioritize usability and performance improvements.

Operational Challenges: Business leaders can identify inefficiencies in current systems, guiding architects to focus on maintainability and scalability.

Building Consensus
Architecture decisions can significantly impact various stakeholders. Engaging them in discussions fosters a sense of ownership and builds consensus around the architectural vision. This collaboration leads to:

Reduced Resistance: When stakeholders are involved in the decision-making process, they are more likely to support the architecture, reducing resistance during implementation.

Better Change Management: Engaging stakeholders early helps identify potential challenges in adopting the new architecture, allowing teams to develop strategies for managing these changes effectively.

Collaborating with Technical Leads: Ensuring Feasibility and Coherence

Technical Insight

Technical leads possess deep knowledge of the technologies and frameworks being used. Engaging them in discussions about architecture qualities ensures that proposed solutions are technically feasible and coherent. This collaboration helps:

Identify Constraints: Technical leads can highlight potential limitations of certain technologies, allowing architects to make informed decisions about which qualities can realistically be prioritized.

Assess Impact: Technical leads can evaluate how architectural decisions will impact the existing codebase, ensuring that proposed changes align with current practices and technologies.

Balancing Trade-offs

In many cases, enhancing one architecture quality may compromise another. For example, increasing security may affect performance, while prioritizing maintainability may impact scalability. Engaging technical leads allows teams to:

Explore Alternatives: Technical leads can propose alternative solutions that achieve a better balance among competing architecture qualities.

Develop Prototypes: Creating prototypes can help assess the implications of architectural decisions, providing tangible insights into how different qualities interact in practice.

Knowledge Transfer
Engaging technical leads in architecture discussions promotes knowledge transfer within the team. This collaborative approach fosters:

Skill Development: Team members can learn from technical leads, improving their understanding of architectural principles and practices.

Shared Responsibility: Involving technical leads ensures that architectural decisions are not solely the responsibility of architects, leading to a more cohesive team dynamic.

Conclusion

Engaging stakeholders and technical leads in discussions about architecture qualities is essential. This collaboration ensures that architectural decisions align with business objectives, address user needs, and remain technically feasible. By fostering open communication and collaboration, teams can make informed decisions that lead to successful software architectures, ultimately resulting in systems that meet user expectations and support organizational goals.

Through these discussions, teams can navigate the complexities of architecture design, balance competing qualities, and build a foundation that supports both current needs and future growth. As a result, organizations will be better equipped to adapt to change and thrive in a competitive landscape.

The Importance of Flexibility in Software Architecture

The importance of flexibility in software architecture cannot be overstated in a rapidly changing technological landscape. As businesses grow, user needs shift, and technology advances, architects must design systems that can adapt to these changes without requiring extensive rework or leading to system failures.

This article explores what flexibility means in software architecture, why it is crucial, and how architects can create flexible architectures to support ongoing evolution.

Understanding Flexibility in Software Architecture

Flexibility in software architecture refers to the ability of a system to adapt to changes in requirements, technologies, and environments with minimal disruption. It encompasses several dimensions, including:

Changeability: The ease with which a system can accommodate changes in requirements or features without significant re-engineering.

Scalability: The capacity to handle increased load or user demands, allowing the system to grow as the business expands.

Interoperability: The ability of different systems or components to work together seamlessly, enabling integration with external services or applications.

Extensibility: The capacity to incorporate new features or functionality without necessitating major rewrites of existing code.

Maintainability: The ease with which a system can be updated or repaired, ensuring that it can evolve alongside changing technologies and user needs.

Flexibility is not merely a desirable quality; it is an essential attribute that enables software systems to remain relevant and effective over time.

The Importance of Flexibility in Software Architecture

Adapting to Change

The fast-paced nature of the business environment means that change is the only constant. Organizations often face shifting market demands, evolving technologies, and new regulatory requirements. A flexible architecture allows businesses to pivot quickly in response to these changes. For instance:

Feature Adjustments: As user feedback emerges, flexible architectures can accommodate new features or modify existing ones without incurring significant costs or delays.

Integration of New Technologies: Organizations may need to adopt new technologies (e.g., cloud computing, artificial intelligence, or blockchain) to remain competitive. Flexible architectures can integrate these technologies smoothly, ensuring continued innovation.

Reducing Technical Debt

Technical debt accumulates when teams take shortcuts or make trade-offs to deliver projects faster.

This debt can lead to rigid architectures that are difficult to change or maintain. By prioritizing flexibility in the architecture, teams can mitigate the risks associated with technical debt, including:

Increased Costs: Systems that are hard to modify often require more time and resources to maintain, leading to escalating operational costs.

Limited Agility: Rigid architectures stifle an organization's ability to respond quickly to new opportunities or threats, hindering overall competitiveness.

Enhancing User Experience

User expectations are continually evolving, and software systems must adapt to provide a satisfactory experience. A flexible architecture allows for:

Rapid Iteration: Teams can quickly implement changes based on user feedback, ensuring the product remains relevant and user-friendly.

Personalization: Flexible architectures enable the implementation of personalized features tailored to individual user preferences, enhancing engagement and satisfaction.

Supporting Diverse Stakeholder Needs

Different stakeholders may have varying requirements, from end-users to business leaders and compliance officers. A flexible architecture can support these diverse needs by:

Modular Design: Architects can design systems using modular components, allowing for easy updates or replacements based on stakeholder input without disrupting the entire system.

Scalable Solutions: As organizations grow, their requirements may evolve. A flexible architecture ensures that systems can scale alongside the business, accommodating increased demands without requiring a complete overhaul.

Designing Flexible Architectures

Embrace Modular Design
Modularity is a foundational principle of flexible architecture. By breaking systems into smaller, independent components, architects can design systems that are easier to modify, test, and maintain. This approach allows teams to:

Isolate Changes: When a change is required, it can often be made in one module without impacting others, reducing the risk of introducing bugs.

Promote Reusability: Modular components can be reused across different projects, reducing development time and costs.

Implement Loose Coupling

Loose coupling refers to minimizing dependencies between components. This design principle enables flexibility by ensuring that changes in one component do not necessitate changes in others. To achieve loose coupling, architects can:

Utilize APIs: Well-defined application programming interfaces (APIs) allow different components to communicate while minimizing direct dependencies.

Adopt Service-Oriented Architecture (SOA): SOA enables components to interact through services, allowing for greater flexibility and easier integration with third-party systems.

Prioritize Extensibility

Architects should design systems with extensibility in mind, allowing for the seamless addition of new features or integrations. Strategies for achieving extensibility include:

Use of Plugins: Implementing a plugin architecture allows developers to add new functionality without altering the core system, promoting flexibility and innovation.

Adopt Microservices: Microservices architecture facilitates the development of small, independently deployable services that can be scaled or modified as needed, enhancing system flexibility.

Focus on Continuous Integration and Deployment (CI/CD)

Adopting CI/CD practices fosters an environment where software can be continuously updated and improved. This approach allows for:

Rapid Feedback Loops: Frequent integration and testing enable teams to identify issues early and iterate quickly, promoting a flexible development process.

Streamlined Deployment: Automated deployment processes reduce the time and effort required to release updates, enabling organizations to respond swiftly to changes.

Engage in Active Communication

Effective communication among stakeholders, developers, and architects is critical for maintaining flexibility in architecture. By fostering open dialogue, teams can:

Align on Requirements: Regular communication ensures that all parties understand the evolving needs of the business and users, enabling architects to design systems that remain adaptable.

Facilitate Knowledge Sharing: Collaborative environments encourage knowledge sharing and collective problem-solving, promoting innovative solutions and enhancing overall flexibility.

Conclusion

Flexibility is an essential characteristic of modern software architecture, enabling systems to adapt to change, reduce technical debt, enhance user experiences, and support diverse stakeholder needs. By prioritizing principles such as modular design, loose coupling, extensibility, continuous integration, and effective communication, architects can create systems that remain relevant and responsive in a rapidly changing technological landscape.

As businesses continue to navigate complex challenges and opportunities, flexible architectures will play a pivotal role in ensuring long-term success. By designing with flexibility in mind, architects not only safeguard the future of their software systems but also empower organizations to thrive in an ever-evolving market.

Understanding Understandability in Software Architectures

Understandability is a critical quality of software architectures that significantly impacts the success of software projects. It refers to the ease with which stakeholders—developers, architects, project managers, and even end-users—can comprehend the architecture's structure, purpose, and design decisions. A software architecture that is easy to understand promotes effective communication, efficient collaboration, and ultimately leads to higher-quality systems.

Why Understandability Matters

Facilitates Communication

Software projects often involve diverse teams with varying levels of expertise. An understandable architecture allows team members to communicate effectively about design decisions, system components, and interactions. Clear documentation and visual representations, such as architecture diagrams, help bridge the knowledge gap among stakeholders, enabling smoother collaboration.

Enhances Collaboration

When architects create understandable architectures, they foster an environment where developers can easily grasp how components interact. This understanding encourages collaboration, as team members feel more confident discussing issues, suggesting improvements, and proposing changes. It reduces the likelihood of misunderstandings that can lead to costly errors and rework.

Promotes Maintainability

Software systems are not static; they require ongoing maintenance and updates. An understandable architecture enables developers to navigate the codebase more easily, making it simpler to identify areas for improvement or bug fixes. When new team members join the project, an easily understandable architecture accelerates their onboarding process, reducing the time required to become productive contributors.

Supports Decision-Making

Understandable architectures provide a clear framework for evaluating design choices and trade-offs. Stakeholders can assess how different architectural decisions impact performance, scalability, and maintainability. This clarity empowers teams to make informed decisions that align with business goals and user needs.

Characteristics of Understandable Architectures

Clarity

Architecture should be clearly defined and documented, using consistent terminology and straightforward language. Avoiding jargon and overly complex explanations ensures that all stakeholders can grasp the essential concepts.

Simplicity

Complex architectures can lead to confusion and misinterpretation. Striving for simplicity in design — such as modular components and clear interfaces — enhances understandability. Simple architectures are easier to visualize and reason about, making it simpler for teams to comprehend how the system functions.

Visual Representation

Diagrams and visual models, such as C4 diagrams or UML, play a crucial role in enhancing understandability. These representations provide an at-a-glance view of the architecture, illustrating how components interact and fit together. Visuals should be clear and accessible, avoiding clutter and overly abstract representations.

Documentation

Comprehensive and well-organized documentation is essential for fostering understandability. It should include descriptions of architectural decisions, design patterns, and rationale behind choices made during the development process. Regularly updated documentation ensures that changes in the architecture are reflected, keeping all stakeholders informed.

Conclusion

Understandability is a foundational quality in software architectures that directly influences communication, collaboration, maintainability, and decision-making. By prioritizing clarity, simplicity, visual representation, and robust documentation, architects can create systems that are not only effective but also easy for all stakeholders to understand. In doing so, organizations can enhance project success, improve team dynamics, and ensure their software systems remain adaptable to future needs.

Testability in Software Architecture: Designing for Success

Testability is a crucial aspect of software architecture that directly impacts the quality and reliability of software systems. It refers to the ease with which a system can be tested to ensure it meets its specified requirements and functions correctly. By emphasizing testability in the architectural design phase, teams can identify issues early, reduce the cost of fixes, and improve overall software quality.

The Importance of Testability

Early Detection of Defects
A well-architected system that is designed with testability in mind allows for early detection of defects and issues.

By incorporating testing into the development process from the outset, teams can identify problems before they escalate, leading to significant cost savings and reduced development time. Early testing also ensures that the system aligns with business requirements and user expectations.

Facilitating Automated Testing
Automated testing is crucial for ensuring software quality in the fast-paced development environment.
Testable architectures support the implementation of automated tests, enabling continuous integration and continuous delivery (CI/CD) practices.

This approach allows for frequent validation of the system against requirements, ensuring that new features or changes do not introduce regressions.

Enhancing Maintainability

Testability and maintainability go hand in hand. A system designed for easy testing is often easier to maintain.

Clear separation of concerns, modular design, and well-defined interfaces simplify the testing process and allow developers to identify and resolve issues more quickly.
When changes are made, testable architectures help ensure that existing functionality remains intact, reducing the risk of introducing new defects.

Boosting Team Confidence

A testable architecture instills confidence in the development team. Knowing that there are comprehensive tests in place allows developers to make changes and experiment with new features without fear of breaking existing functionality.

This confidence encourages innovation and agility, as teams are more willing to iterate and improve the software.

Designing for Testability

Modular Design

Creating a modular architecture enables the separation of concerns, allowing individual components to be tested independently.

Each module can have its own set of tests, making it easier to isolate and identify issues.

This approach not only improves testability but also enhances maintainability and reusability.

Dependency Injection
Utilizing dependency injection techniques helps decouple components, making them easier to test in isolation. By injecting dependencies rather than hardcoding them, architects can create a flexible system that allows for easy swapping of implementations. This enables the use of mock objects or stubs during testing, facilitating more controlled and effective test scenarios.

Clear Interfaces
Well-defined interfaces are essential for testability. They provide a clear contract for how components interact, making it easier to verify that each component behaves as expected. Architects should design interfaces that are easy to understand and implement, simplifying the process of writing tests.

Embrace Testing Principles
Adopting testing principles such as the Single Responsibility Principle (SRP) and the Open/Closed Principle (OCP) can enhance testability. SRP encourages components to have one clear purpose, while OCP allows for the extension of behavior without modifying existing code. These principles lead to simpler, more testable codebases.

Conclusion

Testability is a vital quality in software architecture that should be prioritized during the design phase. By emphasizing testability through modular design, dependency injection, clear interfaces, and adherence to testing principles, architects can create systems that are easier to test and maintain. In doing so, organizations can enhance software quality, reduce costs associated with defect resolution, and foster a culture of continuous improvement within development teams. Ultimately, designing for testability ensures that software systems not only meet current requirements but are also adaptable to future changes and challenges.

Speed to Market: The Key to Competitive Advantage

The fast-paced digital landscape has made speed to market a critical factor for business success, especially in the software and technology sectors. Speed to market refers to the time it takes for a product or service to move from the initial concept phase to being available for customers. This concept is vital not only for achieving immediate commercial success but also for maintaining a competitive edge in an ever-evolving marketplace.

Why Speed to Market Matters

Competitive Advantage

In industries characterized by rapid innovation and changing consumer preferences, the ability to quickly launch products can set a company apart from its competitors. Businesses that can bring new features, products, or services to market faster can capture market share, respond to emerging trends, and meet customer demands more effectively. The faster a company can deliver a solution, the better positioned it is to establish itself as a leader in its field.

Customer Satisfaction

Speed to market directly correlates with customer satisfaction. Today's consumers expect timely solutions that address their needs. Companies that can respond quickly to feedback and deliver enhancements or new offerings are more likely to build loyal customer relationships. Moreover, engaging customers early in the development process allows businesses to adapt their offerings to better meet user expectations.

Revenue Generation

Bringing products to market faster enables organizations to generate revenue sooner. This is particularly important in industries where the window for profitability can be narrow. By reducing the time it takes to launch, companies can start earning revenue while competitors are still developing their offerings, maximizing return on investment (ROI) and ensuring sustainability.

Agility and Flexibility

Organizations that prioritize speed to market foster a culture of agility and flexibility. By adopting agile methodologies, such as Scrum or Kanban, teams can respond quickly to changes in requirements or market conditions. This adaptability is crucial in a landscape where technology and consumer preferences are continually evolving.

Strategies to Improve Speed to Market

Agile Development Practices

Implementing agile development methodologies can significantly enhance speed to market. Agile promotes iterative development, allowing teams to deliver small increments of functionality quickly. This enables organizations to gather user feedback continuously, adapt to changing needs, and reduce time wasted on unnecessary features.

Cross-Functional Teams

Creating cross-functional teams that bring together diverse skills — such as development, design, marketing, and sales — can accelerate the product development process.

These teams can collaborate more effectively, streamline decision-making, and ensure that all aspects of the product are aligned with market needs.

Automation and DevOps

Leveraging automation tools and DevOps practices can speed up both development and deployment processes. Automated testing, continuous integration, and continuous delivery (CI/CD) pipelines help reduce manual effort, minimize errors, and ensure a smoother transition from development to production. This efficiency ultimately shortens the overall time to market.

Prioritize Minimum Viable Products (MVP)

Focusing on developing a minimum viable product (MVP) allows teams to launch a basic version of a product quickly. This strategy enables organizations to validate ideas, gather user feedback, and make informed decisions for future iterations. An MVP approach minimizes initial investment and helps identify what features resonate most with users.

Conclusion

Speed to market is a vital component of modern business strategy, influencing competitive advantage, customer satisfaction, revenue generation, and overall organizational agility. By adopting agile methodologies, fostering cross-functional collaboration, leveraging automation, and prioritizing MVPs, businesses can enhance their ability to deliver products quickly and effectively. In an increasingly dynamic marketplace, those that prioritize speed to market will be better positioned to thrive and succeed.

Elasticity and Scalability in Software Architecture: Ensuring Performance and Resource Optimization

The fast-paced digital environment makes the ability of software systems to adapt to varying loads and user demands crucial for maintaining performance and user satisfaction. Elasticity and scalability are two key concepts in software architecture that address how systems respond to changes in workload and how they manage resources effectively. This article will explore the definitions of elasticity and scalability, their importance, key characteristics, and best practices for designing systems that can achieve both.

Understanding Elasticity and Scalability

Elasticity

Elasticity refers to the capability of a system to dynamically adjust its resources in response to changes in demand. This means that a system can automatically scale up or down, adding or removing resources as needed to accommodate varying workloads. Elasticity is particularly important in cloud computing environments, where workloads can fluctuate dramatically based on user activity, seasonal trends, or unexpected events.

Key Characteristics of Elastic Systems:

Dynamic Resource Allocation: Resources can be provisioned or de-provisioned automatically, ensuring that the system has the necessary capacity to handle current demand.

Cost Efficiency: Elastic systems optimize costs by scaling resources based on actual usage, allowing organizations to pay only for what they need.

Responsive Performance: Elasticity enhances user experience by maintaining consistent performance during spikes in traffic or workload.

Scalability

Scalability refers to the ability of a system to handle an increasing amount of workload or to be easily enlarged to accommodate that growth. A scalable system can maintain or improve performance as the number of users or transactions increases. Scalability can be achieved through two primary approaches:

Vertical Scaling (Scaling Up): This involves adding more power (CPU, RAM, etc.) to an existing server to handle increased load. While this approach is straightforward, it has limitations, as there's a maximum capacity for each server.

Horizontal Scaling (Scaling Out): This involves adding more servers or nodes to a system to distribute the load. Horizontal scaling is often more effective for handling large-scale applications, as it allows for better fault tolerance and resource distribution.

Key Characteristics of Scalable Systems:

Performance Consistency: Scalable systems maintain performance levels as they grow, ensuring that response times and throughput remain acceptable.

Resource Efficiency: A scalable architecture allows for optimal utilization of resources, minimizing waste and ensuring that resources are available when needed.

Growth Accommodation: Scalable systems can easily adapt to increasing workloads, whether through additional hardware or more efficient software designs.

Importance of Elasticity and Scalability

Enhanced User Experience
Both elasticity and scalability directly impact user experience. Systems that can adjust to varying loads ensure that users experience minimal latency and downtime, which is crucial for maintaining satisfaction and loyalty.

Cost Management
Organizations face pressure to manage costs while delivering high-quality services. Elasticity allows businesses to optimize resource usage, scaling down when demand decreases and reducing unnecessary expenditures. Scalability enables organizations to grow without over-provisioning resources upfront, ensuring cost-effective expansion.

Business Continuity
The unpredictable market requires businesses to respond quickly to sudden changes in demand, such as seasonal peaks or unexpected traffic spikes. Elastic and scalable architectures help ensure that organizations can maintain operations and service availability during these fluctuations.

Competitive Advantage
Organizations that invest in elastic and scalable systems are better positioned to compete in the market. They can quickly adapt to changes, innovate more rapidly, and deliver new features and capabilities without compromising performance.

Designing for Elasticity and Scalability

Adopt Cloud-Native Principles

Designing applications using cloud-native principles is a key strategy for achieving elasticity and scalability. Cloud-native architectures leverage microservices, containers, and serverless computing to enable dynamic resource allocation and seamless scaling. Key practices include:

Microservices Architecture: Breaking applications into smaller, independently deployable services that can be scaled individually based on demand.

Containers: Using containerization to isolate applications and their dependencies, allowing for consistent deployment and efficient resource usage.

Serverless Computing: Leveraging serverless platforms to automatically scale resources based on demand, eliminating the need for manual provisioning.

Implement Load Balancing

Load balancing distributes incoming traffic across multiple servers or instances, ensuring that no single resource becomes a bottleneck. Implementing load balancers helps achieve both elasticity and scalability by:

Enhancing Performance: By spreading the load evenly, load balancers prevent any single server from becoming overwhelmed, ensuring consistent response times.

Facilitating Horizontal Scaling: Load balancers enable the addition of new instances to the system, allowing for seamless horizontal scaling.

Monitor Performance and Resource Utilization

Continuous monitoring of system performance and resource utilization is essential for maintaining elasticity and scalability. Implementing monitoring tools allows organizations to:

Identify Bottlenecks: Quickly detect areas of the system that are underperforming and require additional resources or optimization.

Optimize Resource Allocation: Adjust resource allocation based on real-time usage patterns, ensuring that resources are allocated efficiently.

Use Automated Scaling

Automated scaling mechanisms enable systems to adjust resources in real-time based on predefined rules or metrics. This includes:

Vertical Scaling Automation: Automatically increasing or decreasing the resources allocated to an instance based on performance metrics such as CPU or memory usage.

Horizontal Scaling Automation: Automatically adding or removing instances based on demand, such as user traffic or transaction volume.

Design for Statelessness

Stateless design principles improve both elasticity and scalability. Stateless applications do not retain information about user sessions or transactions, allowing instances to be easily added or removed without losing context.

This approach simplifies load balancing and scaling, as any instance can handle requests without dependencies on specific data or sessions.

Optimize Data Management

Efficient data management is crucial for maintaining performance in scalable systems. Strategies include:

Data Sharding: Distributing data across multiple databases or storage systems to improve read and write performance.

Caching: Implementing caching mechanisms to store frequently accessed data, reducing the load on databases and improving response times.

Conclusion

Elasticity and scalability are essential characteristics of modern software architectures that ensure systems can adapt to changing workloads and user demands.

By understanding and implementing these concepts, organizations can enhance user experience, optimize costs, and ensure business continuity in an ever-evolving digital landscape.

Designing for elasticity and scalability requires adopting cloud-native principles, implementing load balancing, monitoring performance, using automated scaling, and optimizing data management.

By prioritizing these strategies, architects and developers can build resilient systems capable of delivering consistent performance and effectively responding to fluctuations in demand. As technology continues to advance, embracing elasticity and scalability will be critical for organizations striving to remain competitive and meet the needs of their users.

Reusability: Unlocking Efficiency and Innovation in Software Development

Reusability has emerged as a fundamental principle that drives efficiency, reduces costs, and fosters innovation. Reusability refers to the practice of designing software components, modules, or systems in such a way that they can be used in multiple applications or contexts without significant modification. By emphasizing reusability in software architecture, organizations can streamline their development processes, improve code quality, and accelerate time to market.

Why Reusability Matters

Cost Reduction
One of the most significant benefits of reusability is the potential for cost savings. By reusing existing components, organizations can avoid redundant development efforts, reducing the time and resources spent on creating new features from scratch. This efficiency translates to lower development costs and allows teams to allocate resources to other critical areas of the project.

Faster Time to Market
Reusability enables faster delivery of software products and features. When developers can leverage pre-existing components or libraries, they can focus on higher-level functionality and business logic instead of reinventing the wheel.

This acceleration in development processes allows organizations to bring products to market more quickly, gaining a competitive advantage.

Improved Quality

Reusing well-tested and proven components enhances the overall quality of software systems.

Established components typically have undergone rigorous testing and have demonstrated reliability in previous applications. By incorporating these components into new projects, organizations can reduce the likelihood of introducing bugs and improve the overall stability of the software.

Consistency Across Applications

Reusability fosters consistency across different applications and projects. By using standardized components and libraries, organizations can ensure that similar functionalities behave in the same way across various systems. This consistency not only improves user experience but also simplifies maintenance, as developers become familiar with a common set of components and interfaces.

Strategies to Enhance Reusability

Modular Design

Adopting a modular design approach is essential for promoting reusability. By breaking down applications into smaller, self-contained modules, developers can create components that can be independently developed, tested, and reused across multiple projects.

This modularity encourages a clear separation of concerns, making it easier to understand and manage the codebase.

Use of Libraries and Frameworks
Leveraging libraries and frameworks that promote reusability can significantly enhance development efficiency. Frameworks often provide reusable components for common functionalities, enabling developers to focus on the unique aspects of their applications. By using established libraries, teams can take advantage of community support and regular updates, ensuring that their solutions remain current and secure.

Documentation and Standards
Thorough documentation is crucial for promoting reusability. Clear guidelines on how to use and integrate reusable components ensure that developers understand their functionality and implementation requirements.
Establishing coding standards and conventions can also enhance the readability and maintainability of reusable components, making it easier for teams to adopt them in various contexts.

Design Patterns
Implementing design patterns can improve reusability by providing established solutions to common problems.
Patterns like the Factory, Strategy, or Observer pattern enable developers to create flexible and extensible components that can be reused across different projects. By recognizing and applying these patterns, teams can build a library of reusable solutions that address specific challenges in software development.

Conclusion

Reusability is a powerful principle that enhances efficiency, reduces costs, and improves the quality of software development. By prioritizing modular design, leveraging libraries and frameworks, maintaining thorough documentation, and applying design patterns, organizations can create a robust ecosystem of reusable components. Embracing reusability not only accelerates time to market but also fosters innovation, allowing teams to focus on delivering unique and valuable solutions to their customers. In an increasingly competitive landscape, the ability to reuse and repurpose existing assets will be a significant driver of success for software organizations.

Releasability: The Key to Efficient Software Delivery

Releasability has become an essential aspect of the software lifecycle in the fast-paced world of software development. Releasability refers to the ability of a software product to be deployed into a production environment efficiently, reliably, and with minimal risk. This concept encompasses not only the technical aspects of releasing software but also the processes, practices, and strategies that ensure smooth transitions from development to deployment. Prioritizing releasability organizations to deliver value to customers more effectively and respond to market demands with agility.

Why Releasability Matters

Faster Time to Market
A high level of releasability allows organizations to deliver software products and features to the market more quickly. When teams can streamline the deployment process, they can release updates, fixes, and new functionalities rapidly, ensuring that customers receive the latest improvements without long waiting periods. This speed is crucial in a competitive landscape where customers expect timely solutions.

Reduced Risk of Failures
Effective releasability strategies minimize the risks associated with deploying new software.
By implementing robust testing, continuous integration, and continuous delivery (CI/CD) practices, teams can identify and resolve issues before they reach production.

This proactive approach reduces the likelihood of failures or regressions in live environments, enhancing overall system stability and reliability.

Improved Customer Satisfaction
When organizations prioritize releasability, they can respond quickly to customer feedback and market changes. Frequent releases enable businesses to address user concerns, implement requested features, and deliver enhancements that align with customer expectations. This responsiveness fosters customer satisfaction and loyalty, leading to a more favorable perception of the brand.

Enhanced Team Morale and Collaboration
A well-defined release process encourages collaboration among development, operations, and other stakeholders. When teams understand the releasability goals and workflows, they can work more effectively together, leading to improved communication and collaboration. This alignment enhances team morale as members see the tangible impact of their work in delivering quality software to users.

Strategies to Improve Releasability

Implement Continuous Integration and Continuous Delivery (CI/CD)

Adopting CI/CD practices is one of the most effective ways to enhance releasability. Continuous integration ensures that code changes are integrated and tested regularly, allowing teams to identify issues early. Continuous delivery automates the deployment process, enabling teams to release new features and fixes with minimal manual intervention. Together, these practices lead to more frequent and reliable releases.

Automated Testing

Incorporating automated testing into the development process is crucial for ensuring releasability.

Automated tests can quickly verify that new code does not introduce regressions or break existing functionality.

By running a suite of tests as part of the CI/CD pipeline, teams can gain confidence in the quality of their releases and reduce the risk of defects reaching production.

Feature Toggles

Feature toggles, or flags, allow teams to control the visibility of new features in production. This strategy enables developers to deploy code without immediately exposing new functionalities to users. By using feature toggles, teams can gradually roll out features, gather feedback, and make adjustments before a full-scale release, thereby enhancing overall releasability.

Comprehensive Documentation

Clear and comprehensive documentation is vital for effective releasability.

Documentation should cover the release process, deployment procedures, and any configurations or dependencies required for the software. This clarity helps teams understand their roles in the release process and ensures that everyone is aligned on expectations, reducing the potential for miscommunication or errors.

Conclusion

Releasability is a fundamental aspect of modern software development that directly influences the efficiency and effectiveness of software delivery. By prioritizing releasability through practices such as CI/CD, automated testing, feature toggles, and comprehensive documentation, organizations can enhance their ability to deploy software reliably and responsively. In an environment where customer expectations are continually evolving, fostering a culture of releasability will empower teams to deliver high-quality solutions swiftly and maintain a competitive edge in the marketplace. Ultimately, the ability to release software with confidence is a significant driver of success for any organization striving to meet the demands of today's digital landscape.

Portability: The Key to Flexible Software Solutions

The diverse technological landscape has made software portability an essential characteristic for applications and systems aiming to reach a wide audience and operate across various environments. Portability refers to the ease with which software can be transferred from one environment to another, including different operating systems, hardware architectures, and cloud platforms. By prioritizing portability in software design and development, organizations can enhance their solutions' flexibility and accessibility, ultimately increasing their reach and effectiveness.

Why Portability Matters

Broadens Market Reach
Portability allows organizations to extend their products to a broader market. Software that can run on multiple operating systems (e.g., Windows, macOS, Linux) or platforms (e.g., cloud, on-premises) can attract a more extensive user base. This increased accessibility enhances customer satisfaction and engagement, leading to higher adoption rates and revenue.

Reduces Vendor Lock-In
When software is designed to be portable, organizations can avoid vendor lock-in, which occurs when a company becomes dependent on a specific vendor's tools, technologies, or services. By ensuring portability, businesses can switch vendors or environments with relative ease, maintaining flexibility and avoiding potential disruptions or increased costs associated with being tied to a single provider.

Facilitates Maintenance and Upgrades

Portable software can be more easily maintained and upgraded across different environments. When developers can adapt the same codebase to various platforms without extensive modifications, they can streamline maintenance processes and reduce the time and effort required for updates. This efficiency contributes to the overall sustainability of the software.

Encourages Innovation

By focusing on portability, developers are encouraged to write code that adheres to open standards and best practices. This mindset fosters innovation, as teams explore new technologies and platforms without being constrained by compatibility issues. As a result, organizations can leverage cutting-edge advancements while maintaining the flexibility to deploy across various environments.

Strategies to Enhance Portability

Use Cross-Platform Development Tools
Utilizing cross-platform development frameworks and tools can significantly enhance software portability. Frameworks like **React Native** and **Xamarin** enable developers to write applications that run on multiple platforms using a single codebase. For example, a mobile application developed with React Native can seamlessly function on both iOS and Android devices, ensuring a consistent user experience.

Adhere to Open Standards
Writing software that adheres to open standards promotes portability. For instance, using web technologies like HTML, CSS, and JavaScript enables web applications to run on any device with a compatible web browser, regardless of the underlying operating system. This approach not only improves accessibility but also simplifies the development process by avoiding platform-specific dependencies.

Abstracting Dependencies
Developers can enhance portability by abstracting dependencies. This means minimizing reliance on specific libraries, APIs, or operating system features that may not be available across all environments. For example, instead of using a specific database management system (DBMS) that may only run on certain platforms, developers can utilize Object-Relational Mapping (ORM) tools like **Hibernate** or **Entity Framework** that support multiple databases, thus enabling greater flexibility.

Containerization
Using containerization technologies such as **Docker** can significantly improve software portability.

Containers encapsulate an application and its dependencies into a single package, allowing it to run consistently across different environments. For instance, a web application developed in a Docker container can be deployed on various cloud platforms or local servers without worrying about compatibility issues, ensuring a smooth transition from development to production.

Examples of Portable Software Development

Web Applications: By leveraging HTML5, CSS3, and JavaScript, developers can create web applications that run in any modern browser, regardless of the operating system. For instance, a project management tool built with these technologies can be accessed by users on Windows, macOS, or Linux without modification.

Java Applications: The Java programming language is inherently portable due to its "write once, run anywhere" (WORA) capability. Applications written in Java can run on any device with a Java Virtual Machine (JVM), making it easy to deploy across various platforms. An example would be an enterprise application designed for both desktop and server environments.

Cross-Platform Mobile Apps: Frameworks like **Flutter** allow developers to create mobile applications that run on both iOS and Android devices from a single codebase. An example of this would be a fitness tracking app that provides a consistent user experience across multiple devices.

APIs: Designing APIs that adhere to RESTful principles ensures that they can be accessed and utilized across various platforms and technologies. For instance, a cloud-based service that offers a RESTful API can be consumed by applications developed in different programming languages, increasing its reach and utility.

Conclusion

Portability is a crucial aspect of modern software development that enhances flexibility, broadens market reach, and facilitates maintenance. By adopting strategies such as cross-platform development, adhering to open standards, abstracting dependencies, and utilizing containerization, organizations can create portable solutions that operate seamlessly across diverse environments. In a rapidly evolving technological landscape, prioritizing portability will empower businesses to innovate, adapt, and thrive while ensuring that their software remains accessible and relevant to users everywhere.

Modularity: Enhancing Testability in Software Development

In software development, modularity is a critical design principle that promotes the separation of functionality into distinct, manageable components or modules. Each module represents a specific piece of functionality or a cohesive set of related features, which can be developed, tested, and maintained independently. By embracing modularity, organizations not only improve the overall architecture of their software systems but also significantly enhance testability, leading to more robust and reliable applications.

Why Modularity Matters

Simplifies Understanding
Modularity simplifies the understanding of complex systems by breaking them down into smaller, more manageable parts. Each module can be designed to encapsulate a specific functionality, making it easier for developers and testers to grasp its purpose and behavior. This clarity reduces cognitive load, allowing team members to focus on individual components without being overwhelmed by the intricacies of the entire system.

Encourages Reusability
Modular components can often be reused across different projects or within different parts of the same application. This reusability not only saves development time but also ensures that tested and proven modules are utilized, thereby enhancing overall software quality.

For example, a module for user authentication can be reused in multiple applications, eliminating the need to redevelop and retest the same functionality.

Facilitates Collaboration

When software is organized into modules, different teams or developers can work on separate components concurrently without stepping on each other's toes. This parallel development fosters collaboration and speeds up the overall development process, allowing for more efficient workflows and faster time to market.

The Connection Between Modularity and Testability

Isolated Testing

One of the most significant advantages of modularity is that it allows for isolated testing of individual components. Each module can be tested independently, ensuring that its functionality works as intended without the influence of other parts of the system. This isolation simplifies the testing process and helps to identify defects more quickly.

For example, consider a modular e-commerce application where the payment processing module can be tested independently from the product catalog module. This isolation enables developers to ensure that the payment logic functions correctly before integrating it with the rest of the system.

Easier Debugging

When a system is modular, identifying and fixing bugs becomes more manageable. If a failure occurs within a specific module, developers can focus their debugging efforts on that isolated component rather than sifting through a monolithic codebase. This targeted approach allows for quicker resolution of issues and a more efficient development cycle.

Enhanced Automation

Modularity lends itself well to automated testing practices. Each module can have its own set of unit tests that validate its functionality, making it easier to integrate into a continuous integration/continuous delivery (CI/CD) pipeline. This automation ensures that modules are continuously tested as code changes are made, allowing teams to catch regressions early and maintain high software quality.

For instance, using testing frameworks such as **JUnit** for Java or **pytest** for Python, developers can automate the testing of individual modules, ensuring that any changes made do not introduce new defects.

Improved Test Coverage

When modules are designed with testability in mind, it becomes easier to achieve comprehensive test coverage across the application. Developers can focus on writing tests for each module, ensuring that various scenarios and edge cases are accounted for. This thorough testing ultimately leads to a more reliable and robust software product.

For example, in a modular application, different test cases can be created for user registration, login, and password recovery modules, ensuring that all functionalities are adequately tested.

Support for Behavior-Driven Development (BDD)

Modular design complements methodologies like Behavior-Driven Development (BDD), where tests are defined based on the expected behavior of individual components. By focusing on the desired outcomes of each module, teams can develop tests that guide the implementation and validate that the software meets its requirements.

For instance, a module responsible for sending notifications can be developed and tested based on user stories, ensuring that it behaves as expected under various conditions.

Conclusion

Modularity is a powerful principle in software development that significantly enhances testability. By breaking down complex systems into smaller, manageable components, organizations can simplify understanding, promote reusability, and facilitate collaboration. The ability to isolate testing, streamline debugging, automate testing processes, and achieve improved test coverage makes modularity an invaluable asset in delivering high-quality software.

As software development continues to evolve, embracing modularity will empower teams to create flexible, maintainable, and reliable applications. In an era where quality and speed are paramount, the synergy between modularity and testability will be a key driver of success in the competitive software landscape.

Maintainability: The Cornerstone of Sustainable Software Development

In the realm of software development, maintainability stands as a critical quality attribute that significantly impacts the longevity and effectiveness of applications. Maintainability refers to the ease with which software can be modified to correct defects, improve performance, or adapt to changing requirements. High maintainability ensures that applications can evolve over time, allowing organizations to respond to user needs, technological advancements, and market dynamics effectively. This article explores the importance of maintainability, its key characteristics, and best practices to enhance it in software systems.

Why Maintainability Matters

Adaptability to Change
Software is rarely static; it often needs to evolve in response to user feedback, shifting business priorities, or new regulatory requirements. High maintainability allows organizations to adapt their applications quickly and efficiently. When developers can modify code without extensive effort, they can implement changes faster, ensuring the software remains relevant and valuable to users.

Cost-Effectiveness

The cost of maintaining software can often exceed the initial development costs.

By prioritizing maintainability, organizations can reduce the long-term expenses associated with fixing bugs, adding new features, or updating technology stacks.
A maintainable codebase requires less effort to change, ultimately leading to lower operational costs and improved return on investment.

Enhanced Collaboration
Maintainability fosters a collaborative development environment. When code is organized, well-documented, and adheres to best practices, it becomes easier for new team members to understand and contribute to the project. This collaboration not only improves team efficiency but also helps in retaining knowledge within the organization, mitigating the risks associated with employee turnover.

Improved Software Quality
Maintainability is closely tied to software quality. Code that is easy to maintain is often cleaner, more organized, and adheres to established coding standards. This clarity reduces the likelihood of introducing new defects during updates or modifications. By focusing on maintainability, teams can enhance the overall quality of their software, leading to increased user satisfaction and trust.

Key Characteristics of Maintainable Software

Readability
Readable code is fundamental to maintainability. When developers can easily understand the logic and structure of the code, they can make modifications with confidence.

Clear naming conventions, consistent formatting, and well-structured code contribute to readability. Comments and documentation that explain complex logic or decisions further enhance understanding.

Modularity

As discussed in the context of modularity, dividing software into smaller, independent components is essential for maintainability. Each module can be developed, tested, and modified independently, reducing the complexity of changes. Modularity allows developers to isolate issues and implement fixes without impacting other parts of the system.

Documentation

Comprehensive documentation is crucial for maintaining software effectively. This includes both technical documentation (such as architecture diagrams, API references, and code comments) and user documentation (such as user manuals and FAQs). Well-documented software enables developers to quickly grasp the system's architecture, dependencies, and usage, facilitating efficient maintenance.

Testability

Maintainable software should be designed with testability in mind. Automated tests can help verify that modifications do not introduce new defects, allowing developers to make changes confidently. The presence of unit tests, integration tests, and end-to-end tests not only supports maintainability but also ensures that the software behaves as expected throughout its lifecycle.

Flexibility

Flexible software can adapt to changing requirements with minimal effort.

This flexibility is often achieved through design patterns, configuration options, and extensible architectures. By allowing for easy customization and updates, teams can enhance maintainability and ensure that the software remains aligned with evolving user needs.

Best Practices to Enhance Maintainability

Code Reviews
Regular code reviews promote maintainability by ensuring adherence to coding standards and best practices. Peer reviews help identify potential issues, improve code quality, and encourage knowledge sharing among team members. This collaborative process fosters a culture of quality and continuous improvement.

Refactoring
Encouraging developers to refactor code regularly is essential for maintaining a clean codebase. Refactoring involves restructuring existing code without changing its external behavior, improving readability, and reducing complexity. By investing time in refactoring, teams can enhance maintainability and prevent the accumulation of technical debt.

Continuous Integration and Continuous Deployment (CI/CD)
Implementing CI/CD pipelines supports maintainability by automating the testing and deployment processes. By continuously integrating code changes and running automated tests, teams can identify and address issues early in the development cycle. This proactive approach helps maintain software quality and minimizes the risk of introducing defects during updates.

Training and Knowledge Sharing
Investing in training and knowledge sharing among team members is vital for maintaining software effectively. When developers are equipped with the latest tools, technologies, and best practices, they can contribute more effectively to the maintainability of the codebase. Regular workshops, knowledge-sharing sessions, and mentorship programs foster a culture of learning and improvement.

Use of Design Patterns

Utilizing established design patterns can enhance maintainability by providing proven solutions to common problems. Patterns such as MVC (Model-View-Controller) or Observer promote clear separation of concerns and improve code organization. By following these patterns, developers can create software that is easier to understand and modify.

Conclusion

Maintainability is a cornerstone of sustainable software development that significantly impacts the long-term success of applications. By prioritizing maintainability, organizations can enhance adaptability, reduce costs, foster collaboration, and improve overall software quality. Characteristics such as readability, modularity, documentation, testability, and flexibility are essential for achieving maintainable code. By adopting best practices like code reviews, refactoring, CI/CD, training, and design patterns, teams can create software that stands the test of time and evolves seamlessly to meet changing needs. Ultimately, a strong focus on maintainability will empower organizations to deliver high-quality software that continues to provide value to users and stakeholders alike.

Loose Coupling vs. Tight Coupling in Software Architecture

In software architecture, the terms "loose coupling" and "tight coupling" describe the relationships between different components or modules within a system. Understanding these concepts is essential for designing flexible, maintainable, and scalable software applications. This article will explore the characteristics, advantages, and disadvantages of loose and tight coupling, along with best practices for achieving an optimal balance between the two.

What is Tight Coupling?

Tight coupling occurs when components in a system are highly dependent on each other. In a tightly coupled architecture, changes in one component often require changes in another, leading to a cascade of modifications throughout the system. This dependency can manifest in various ways, such as:

Direct References: One module directly references or calls functions in another, making them interdependent.

Shared State: Components share data or state, leading to unintended side effects when one component modifies that state.

Inflexible Interfaces: Interfaces between components are rigid, making it difficult to replace or modify individual modules without impacting the entire system.

Advantages of Tight Coupling

Simplicity: For small applications or systems, tight coupling can simplify interactions between components, reducing the complexity of managing relationships.

Performance: Tight coupling may lead to performance optimizations due to reduced overhead from abstractions and indirection.

Disadvantages of Tight Coupling

Reduced Flexibility: Tightly coupled components can be challenging to modify or replace, leading to higher costs and longer development times for updates.

Increased Risk of Bugs: Changes in one component can introduce bugs in other components, making the system more prone to failures.

Difficulties in Testing: Unit testing tightly coupled components can be problematic, as isolating individual components for testing becomes difficult.

What is Loose Coupling?

Loose coupling refers to a design approach where components have minimal dependencies on each other. In a loosely coupled architecture, components interact through well-defined interfaces, allowing them to evolve independently. This independence fosters flexibility and maintainability in the system.

Characteristics of loose coupling include:

Decoupled Interfaces: Components communicate through abstract interfaces, allowing for changes without affecting dependent modules.

Message Passing: Components may communicate via events, messages, or API calls, rather than direct calls, reducing dependencies.

Modularity: Loosely coupled components can be added, removed, or replaced without significant impact on the overall system.

Advantages of Loose Coupling

Increased Flexibility: Loose coupling allows developers to change or replace components independently, facilitating easier updates and modifications.

Enhanced Maintainability: Systems designed with loose coupling are easier to understand, maintain, and extend, reducing the risk of introducing bugs during modifications.

Simplified Testing: Loosely coupled components can be tested in isolation, making unit testing more straightforward and effective.

Disadvantages of Loose Coupling

Complexity: Implementing loose coupling may introduce complexity in terms of managing interfaces and communication between components.

Performance Overhead: The abstractions and indirection required for loose coupling can introduce performance overhead, particularly in systems with high-frequency interactions.

Choosing Between Loose and Tight Coupling

The choice between loose and tight coupling depends on various factors, including the size and complexity of the application, the expected rate of change, and performance requirements. Here are some guidelines to consider:

Consider the Application Size

For small applications with limited functionality, tight coupling may simplify development and reduce overhead.

However, as the application grows, the limitations of tight coupling often become apparent.

For larger applications, loose coupling is generally preferable, as it allows for better scalability and maintainability.

Evaluate Change Frequency

If the application is expected to evolve frequently based on user feedback or changing requirements, loose coupling is essential to enable flexibility.

For stable applications with minimal anticipated changes, tight coupling may suffice.

Balance Performance and Maintainability

In performance-critical applications, some level of tight coupling may be acceptable to optimize interactions. However, it's important to assess whether the performance gains outweigh the maintainability costs.

In most cases, maintainability and flexibility should take precedence over minor performance optimizations.

Best Practices for Achieving Loose Coupling

Use Interfaces and Abstractions: Define clear interfaces that components can implement. This allows components to interact without needing to know the details of each other's implementations.

Implement Design Patterns: Utilize design patterns such as Dependency Injection, Observer, or Publish-Subscribe to facilitate loose coupling. These patterns promote decoupled interactions between components.

Adopt Event-Driven Architecture: Consider an event-driven approach where components communicate through events rather than direct calls. This reduces dependencies and allows components to operate independently.

Encapsulate Functionality: Design components to encapsulate specific functionality and expose only what is necessary through well-defined interfaces. This limits dependencies on internal details and promotes modularity.

Continuous Refactoring: Regularly review and refactor code to maintain loose coupling as the system evolves. This practice ensures that the architecture remains adaptable and aligned with changing requirements.

Conclusion

Understanding the concepts of loose coupling and tight coupling is crucial for effective software architecture. While tight coupling can simplify development in small applications, it often leads to increased complexity and reduced flexibility in larger systems. In contrast, loose coupling promotes adaptability, maintainability, and easier testing, making it the preferred choice for most software applications.

By employing best practices and carefully considering the balance between loose and tight coupling, architects and developers can create robust, flexible systems capable of evolving with the needs of users and the organization. Ultimately, the choice between coupling styles should align with the application's goals, complexity, and anticipated change frequency, ensuring a sustainable and effective software architecture.

Fail-Safe and Fault-Tolerant Software Architectures: Ensuring Reliability in Critical Systems

The digital landscape is seeing software systems become increasingly complex, often needing to operate under stringent reliability and availability demands. Fail-safe and fault-tolerant architectures play a crucial role in ensuring that applications can withstand failures without compromising their functionality or safety. This article will explore the concepts of fail-safe and fault-tolerant architectures, their importance, key characteristics, and best practices for designing systems that can maintain operations in the face of unexpected failures.

Understanding Fail-Safe and Fault-Tolerant Architectures

Fail-Safe Architecture

Fail-safe architecture refers to a design approach that prioritizes safety in the event of a failure.

The primary goal of fail-safe systems is to ensure that when a failure occurs, the system defaults to a safe state, preventing any potential harm to users, data, or the environment. This approach is particularly important in industries where safety is critical, such as aerospace, automotive, healthcare, and industrial control systems.

Key Characteristics of Fail-Safe Architectures:
Safe Defaults: The system is designed to revert to a default state that does not pose risks when an error occurs.
Graceful Degradation: The system continues to operate, albeit at a reduced capacity or with limited functionality, rather than failing completely.

Fail-Safe Mechanisms: Specific mechanisms, such as backup systems or redundant components, are in place to ensure that safety is maintained during failures.

Fault-Tolerant Architecture

Fault-tolerant architecture focuses on maintaining system functionality despite the occurrence of faults or errors. Unlike fail-safe systems that prioritize safety, fault-tolerant designs aim to ensure continuous operation, even in the presence of failures. This approach is critical for applications requiring high availability, such as financial systems, telecommunications, and cloud-based services.

Key Characteristics of Fault-Tolerant Architectures:
Redundancy: Multiple components or systems perform the same function, allowing for seamless failover if one component fails.

Error Detection and Correction: Built-in mechanisms detect faults and either correct them or reroute processes to ensure continued operation.

Self-Healing Capabilities: The system can automatically recover from errors without human intervention, ensuring minimal disruption.

Importance of Fail-Safe and Fault-Tolerant Architectures

Enhanced Reliability
Both fail-safe and fault-tolerant architectures contribute to increased reliability in software systems. By designing systems that can handle failures gracefully, organizations can maintain consistent performance and reduce the risk of downtime.

Improved User Trust
In mission-critical applications, users expect systems to perform reliably under various conditions. Fail-safe and fault-tolerant designs instill confidence in users, assuring them that the system will prioritize their safety and data integrity.

Compliance with Regulatory Standards
Many industries are subject to strict regulatory requirements regarding safety and reliability. Implementing fail-safe and fault-tolerant architectures can help organizations meet these standards and avoid costly penalties.

Business Continuity
Downtime can have severe financial implications for organizations. By adopting fault-tolerant designs, businesses can ensure that their operations continue even in the face of unexpected failures, thereby minimizing potential revenue losses.

Designing Fail-Safe and Fault-Tolerant Architectures

Assess Risk and Impact
Before designing a fail-safe or fault-tolerant system, organizations should conduct a thorough risk assessment to identify potential failure modes and their impact on the system.

This assessment will help prioritize which components require redundancy and what safety measures need to be implemented.

Implement Redundancy

Redundancy is a core principle of both fail-safe and fault-tolerant architectures. Organizations can implement redundancy at various levels:

Hardware Redundancy: Using multiple physical devices to perform the same function, ensuring that if one fails, others can take over.

Software Redundancy: Implementing duplicate software components that can handle the same tasks, allowing for automatic failover in case of failure.

Data Redundancy: Regularly backing up data and maintaining multiple copies in different locations to prevent data loss.

Design for Graceful Degradation

Graceful degradation allows systems to continue operating at a reduced capacity when failures occur. This approach involves identifying critical functionalities and designing the system to maintain those functionalities, even if other parts of the system become unavailable. For instance, a cloud-based application may still allow users to access cached data even if the live database is down.

Implement Robust Error Handling

Effective error handling mechanisms are essential for detecting faults and initiating recovery processes. These mechanisms can include:

Monitoring and Alerting: Continuously monitoring system performance and automatically alerting administrators to potential issues.

Fallback Procedures: Defining fallback procedures that outline how the system should respond to specific types of failures.

Self-Recovery Mechanisms: Designing the system to automatically attempt to recover from errors, such as restarting failed services or rerouting traffic.

Testing and Validation

Thorough testing is critical for ensuring that fail-safe and fault-tolerant architectures function as intended. Organizations should conduct stress tests, fault injection tests, and disaster recovery drills to validate the system's ability to handle failures. Regular testing helps identify weaknesses in the architecture and ensures that the necessary mechanisms are in place to maintain safety and availability.

Continuous Improvement

Software systems and their operating environments are constantly evolving. Organizations should adopt a culture of continuous improvement, regularly reviewing and updating their fail-safe and fault-tolerant mechanisms in response to changing requirements, emerging technologies, and lessons learned from past incidents.

Conclusion

Fail-safe and fault-tolerant architectures are essential for designing reliable software systems that can withstand failures while prioritizing safety and continuous operation. By understanding the differences between these two approaches and implementing best practices such as redundancy, graceful degradation, robust error handling, and thorough testing, organizations can create systems that instill user trust and ensure business continuity. As software applications become increasingly critical to daily operations across various industries, investing in fail-safe and fault-tolerant designs is more important than ever for safeguarding users, data, and organizational interests.

Navigating Legacy Challenges: A New Software Team's Journey

The Transition
In a bustling tech hub, a new software team was formed within a prominent company known for its innovative solutions. The team was tasked with the daunting responsibility of taking over legacy projects from an existing team that had disbanded. Among these projects was a critical web application that served as the company's public-facing website. The stakes were high; the website was not only a key marketing tool but also a vital resource for clients and partners.

However, as the new team delved into the project, they were confronted with an array of challenges that would test their resolve and skills.

The Legacy Monolith
The existing website was built as a monolith, a design choice that, while common in the early days of web development, posed significant hurdles for modern software practices. The structure was riddled with complexities that made it nearly impossible to navigate effectively.

Low Testability and Debuggability
One of the most glaring issues was the website's low testability. The absence of properly defined APIs meant that the team had to contend with HTML calls that returned entire HTML pages instead of structured data. This design choice not only hindered automated testing but also made it challenging to develop unit tests for individual components. As a result, the team faced an uphill battle when attempting to validate changes or enhancements to the website.

Debugging was equally problematic. The original team had utilized Perl for the project, a language that, while powerful, was not implemented with best practices in mind. The code was a tangled web of poorly structured logic, which made tracing errors a frustrating endeavor. The misuse of object-oriented concepts further compounded these difficulties, leading to a lack of reusable components and an overreliance on hardcoded sunny-day scenarios. Instead of a flexible, generic implementation that could adapt to various conditions, the codebase was a rigid structure that required extensive human effort to modify or expand.

Missing Documentation

As the new team sifted through the code, they quickly discovered the absence of comprehensive documentation. Key architecture details were missing, leaving the team in the dark about how different components interacted. Without this context, understanding the system's intricacies became a daunting task. They relied heavily on tribal knowledge from a few remaining staff members who had worked on the project, but this knowledge was limited and often incomplete.

High Maintenance Costs

The costs of maintaining such a poorly designed system became increasingly apparent. Each change required a significant investment of time and resources, often resulting in frustration among team members. Simple updates could take days to implement, leading to delays in delivering critical features. Additionally, the website's high keep-alive cost due to the inefficient codebase strained the budget, further emphasizing the need for a more sustainable solution.

Low Observability

To compound these challenges, the website had low observability.

The lack of effective monitoring tools meant that the team had limited visibility into performance issues or user behavior. This obscured their ability to identify and address problems before they escalated, leading to a reactive rather than proactive approach to maintenance.

The Path Forward: Greenfield Project
As the team grappled with these significant challenges, they realized that continuing to patch and maintain the existing codebase would be a futile endeavor. The only viable solution was to refactor the project from scratch, adopting a greenfield approach.

Understanding Customer Needs
The first step in this transformative journey was to understand customer needs. The team-initiated discussions with stakeholders, gathering requirements and feedback to ensure that the new design would address the pain points that user had experienced with the legacy system.

They conducted user interviews and surveys, focusing on key areas such as functionality, performance, and ease of use. These insights informed the new architecture, guiding decisions that prioritized testability, debuggability, and reliability from the outset.

Designing for Modern Practices
The team set out to design a modern architecture that embraced best practices in software development. They decided to adopt a microservices architecture, which would allow for better modularity and separation of concerns. This approach not only enhanced testability but also facilitated easier debugging, as each service could be developed, tested, and deployed independently. Defining clear APIs was a top priority, ensuring that each microservice communicated effectively and returned structured data. This not only improved automated testing capabilities but also provided a more consistent interface for the front end, paving the way for a smoother user experience.

Embracing a New Technology Stack

Recognizing the limitations of the existing Perl implementation, the team opted for a more modern technology stack. They evaluated various programming languages and frameworks, ultimately choosing one that promoted best practices and community support. This decision facilitated better code organization, improved readability, and enhanced overall maintainability.

Documentation and Continuous Improvement

The importance of documentation became a cornerstone of their new approach. The team adopted a practice of documenting architecture decisions, design patterns, and code implementations thoroughly. This transparency not only helped new team members onboard more effectively but also served as a reference for future enhancements.

In addition, the team integrated observability tools into the new architecture. These tools provided real-time insights into performance metrics and user interactions, enabling the team to respond proactively to potential issues.

Conclusion

As the new software team embarked on their journey to transform a troubled legacy project, they faced significant challenges stemming from low testability, poor debuggability, and a lack of documentation. However, through a commitment to understanding customer needs, embracing modern software practices, and prioritizing documentation, they laid the foundation for a robust, maintainable system. By refactoring the project from scratch, the team not only improved the website's reliability but also fostered a culture of continuous improvement and adaptability. Their experience serves as a valuable reminder of the importance of thoughtful design and documentation in the software development lifecycle,
particularly when navigating the complexities of legacy systems.

The Impact of Clear Architecture on Team Ramp-Up and Productivity

In the world of software development, the ability to onboard new team members efficiently is crucial for maintaining momentum and achieving project goals. A clear and well-structured architecture plays a pivotal role in this process, even in the absence of extensive documentation. This article explores how a clean architecture can facilitate the ramp-up of new developers, including students and interns, and help them become productive contributors in a short time frame. Additionally, we will discuss the concept of cognitive complexity and its implications for the long-term sustainability of software projects.

The Importance of Clear Architecture

Reducing Learning Overhead

When a new team member joins a software project, they often face a steep learning curve. This is particularly true in complex systems where the codebase is intertwined with intricate dependencies, and architectural decisions are obscured by a lack of clarity. However, when a project is built upon a clear architecture, new team members can more easily understand how the various components fit together. This clarity reduces the cognitive load required to grasp the system's functionality and design.

For instance, a well-defined architecture often utilizes established patterns and practices that are familiar to developers, such as Model-View-Controller (MVC) or microservices. These patterns provide a mental framework that new team members can quickly relate to, allowing them to focus on local changes rather than trying to learn the entire project.

Focus on Local Changes

When a software project has a clear architecture, team members can concentrate on specific areas of the codebase without feeling overwhelmed by the complexity of the entire system. This is particularly beneficial for students and junior developers who may not yet have the experience or confidence to navigate a large and convoluted project.

By clearly delineating responsibilities within the architecture, developers can easily identify which components they need to work on.

For example, if a project follows a modular architecture, a new team member can focus solely on the module they are assigned, making changes and enhancements without worrying about unintended consequences in unrelated areas. This focused approach allows for a more manageable learning experience and accelerates the onboarding process.

Enhancing Collaboration

Clear architecture fosters better collaboration among team members. When the system's structure is easily understood, new developers can more easily communicate ideas and seek help from experienced colleagues. This environment enhances learning and encourages knowledge sharing, which is essential for building a cohesive team. As new team members contribute to the codebase, they can implement features or fixes that align with established architectural principles, reinforcing a shared understanding and promoting consistency across the codebase.

Cognitive Complexity: A Key Concept

What is Cognitive Complexity?

Cognitive complexity refers to the mental effort required to understand a system, code, or design. It encompasses the intricacies of the architecture, the relationships between components, and the overall clarity of the code.

High cognitive complexity can lead to confusion and increased errors, while low cognitive complexity promotes understanding and efficient problem-solving.

In the context of software development, cognitive complexity is a critical factor influencing the long-term sustainability of a project. When new team members can quickly grasp the architecture and code, they can make meaningful contributions without being bogged down by confusion or misunderstandings.

Reducing Cognitive Load

By prioritizing clear architecture, teams can significantly reduce cognitive load for new developers. This reduction enables them to ramp up quickly and become productive members of the team in less than a month. For students and junior developers, this is especially beneficial, as they often have limited experience and may struggle with more complex systems.

The benefits of reducing cognitive complexity extend beyond onboarding. As team members become familiar with the architecture and codebase, they can identify areas for improvement and propose enhancements more effectively. This proactive approach contributes to the long-term health of the project, as developers continuously refine and optimize the system.

The Long-Term Impact of Clear Architecture
A clear architecture not only facilitates the ramp-up of new team members but also ensures the longevity of the software project. Here are some of the key benefits:

Easier Maintenance: A well-structured system is easier to maintain, as developers can quickly identify issues and implement fixes. This reduces technical debt and helps prevent the codebase from becoming unmanageable over time.

Improved Adaptability: Software projects often evolve over time, requiring changes to accommodate new features or shifting business requirements. Clear architecture allows teams to adapt more easily to these changes, as the impact on the overall system can be assessed with greater clarity.

Enhanced Knowledge Transfer: When a project has a clean architecture, knowledge transfer becomes more effective. If a developer leaves the team or if new members join, the existing architecture serves as a solid foundation for onboarding. This continuity reduces the risk of losing critical knowledge and helps ensure that the project remains on track.

Greater Team Morale: Teams that experience smooth onboarding processes and reduced frustration due to cognitive overload tend to have higher morale. A positive work environment fosters creativity and innovation, leading to better outcomes for the project.

Conclusion

Clear architecture plays a vital role in facilitating the ramp-up of new team members, including students and junior developers. By reducing cognitive complexity, a well-structured system enables developers to focus on local changes and become productive contributors in a short timeframe. The benefits of prioritizing clear architecture extend beyond onboarding; they enhance collaboration, improve maintainability, and contribute to the long-term sustainability of the software project.

As organizations strive to attract and retain talent, the importance of creating clear and accessible architectures cannot be overstated. By investing in clean architecture, teams can ensure that new members feel welcomed and empowered, fostering a culture of collaboration and continuous improvement that will benefit the project for years to come.

The Impact of Team-Level Accepted Rules for Coding, Quality and Culture on Software Projects

A team's effectiveness and efficiency are crucial to a project's success in the fast-paced world of software development. Key to this success is establishing accepted rules for coding, quality standards, and a positive team culture. These elements contribute to technical success while fostering collaboration, innovation, and long-term sustainability. This chapter explores the impact of these team-level rules and how they shape software projects from start to finish.

Establishing Coding Standards

Importance of Coding Standards

Coding standards are guidelines that dictate how code should be written and organized within a project. These standards serve multiple purposes:

Consistency: Consistent coding practices make it easier for team members to read and understand each other's code. When everyone adheres to the same standards, the cognitive load required to comprehend unfamiliar code decreases, allowing developers to focus on functionality rather than deciphering style discrepancies.

Maintainability: Well-structured and uniformly styled code is easier to maintain. If coding standards are in place, new developers can quickly adapt to the codebase, making it simpler to add features or fix bugs without inadvertently introducing new issues.

Collaboration: Team members often collaborate on code, whether through pair programming, code reviews, or shared responsibilities. Clear coding standards facilitate smoother collaboration by reducing misunderstandings and aligning team members on how to approach code development.

Benefits of Coding Standards in Software Projects

When a team adopts coding standards, the impact is evident in the overall quality of the software. Benefits include:

Reduced Bugs: By following established patterns and practices, developers can minimize the likelihood of errors and bugs in the code. Consistent use of naming conventions, indentation, and documentation can make it easier to spot anomalies.

Faster Onboarding: New team members can ramp up more quickly when coding standards are in place. They spend less time trying to understand varying code styles and more time becoming productive contributors.

Enhanced Code Reviews: Code reviews become more effective when team members are familiar with the coding standards. Reviewers can focus on the logic and functionality of the code rather than getting bogged down by stylistic concerns.

Commitment to Quality

Defining Quality Standards

Quality standards encompass various aspects of software development, including performance, reliability, security, and user experience. By setting clear expectations for quality, teams can ensure that they deliver products that meet or exceed stakeholder requirements.

Testing Protocols: Establishing protocols for unit testing, integration testing, and end-to-end testing is essential. These protocols define how and when tests should be performed, ensuring that quality is baked into the development process.

Code Review Processes: A culture of regular code reviews can help maintain quality standards. By having peers evaluate each other's code, teams can identify potential issues early and promote knowledge sharing.

Performance Metrics: Defining key performance indicators (KPIs) for software projects can help teams measure and evaluate their success. These metrics might include response times, uptime percentages, or user satisfaction scores.

The Impact of Quality Standards on Software Projects

Implementing quality standards can have a transformative effect on software projects:

Improved Reliability: Consistent quality checks and testing practices lead to more reliable software. This reliability is essential for maintaining user trust and satisfaction, particularly in production environments.

Enhanced User Experience: By focusing on quality, teams can create products that deliver exceptional user experiences. This focus on user-centered design can lead to higher adoption rates and positive feedback.

Long-Term Cost Savings: Investing in quality upfront can save significant costs down the line. Addressing issues during development is often less expensive than fixing problems after deployment.

Fostering a Positive Team Culture

Building a Strong Team Culture
A positive team culture is characterized by collaboration, respect, and shared values. When team members feel valued and engaged, they are more likely to contribute their best efforts to the project. Key elements of a strong team culture include:

Open Communication: Encouraging open dialogue fosters an environment where team members feel comfortable sharing ideas, raising concerns, and providing feedback.

Recognition and Support: Recognizing individual and team achievements boosts morale and motivates members to perform at their best. Additionally, offering support for professional development helps individuals grow and enhances team capabilities.

Shared Goals: Establishing common goals aligns the team's efforts and reinforces a sense of purpose. When everyone understands the project's objectives, they can work together more effectively to achieve them.

The Impact of Team Culture on Software Projects

A positive team culture can have far-reaching effects on software projects:

Increased Productivity: Teams that feel supported and engaged are more productive. They are likely to go above and beyond in their work, resulting in higher-quality output.

Enhanced Innovation: A culture that encourages experimentation and risk-taking can lead to innovative solutions. When team members feel safe to share their ideas, creativity flourishes, leading to unique and effective solutions to challenges.

Improved Employee Retention: Teams that prioritize culture and engagement tend to retain employees longer. High retention rates lead to greater continuity within the team, preserving knowledge and expertise.

Conclusion

The establishment of team-level accepted rules for coding, quality, and culture has a profound impact on the success of software projects. By implementing clear coding standards, teams enhance maintainability and collaboration, while commitment to quality ensures the delivery of reliable, user-friendly software. Furthermore, fostering a positive team culture cultivates an environment where team members feel valued and engaged, leading to increased productivity and innovation.

As software development continues to evolve, the importance of these foundational elements cannot be overstated. Teams that prioritize accepted rules in coding, quality, and culture position themselves for long-term success, ultimately delivering higher-quality products that meet and exceed stakeholder expectations. In a landscape where adaptability and responsiveness are critical, the benefits of a strong team foundation are invaluable, paving the way for sustained growth and achievement in software development.

The Risks and Costs of Infrequent Rebase and Merge in Git

In modern software development, collaboration among team members is essential for creating high-quality applications. Git, as a widely used version control system, provides tools like rebasing and merging to help manage changes made by multiple developers. However, failing to perform these operations frequently can introduce significant risks and costs to a project. This article explores the implications of infrequent rebasing and merging, focusing on the risks associated with code conflicts, integration issues, and overall project inefficiencies.

Understanding Git Rebase and Merge

What is Git Rebase?
Git rebase is a command that allows developers to integrate changes from one branch into another by applying the changes made in the feature branch on top of the target branch. This process results in a linear commit history, which can make the history easier to read and understand. Rebasing is particularly useful for maintaining a clean project history, as it allows developers to avoid unnecessary merge commits.

What is Git Merge?
Git merge is another command that integrates changes from one branch into another but does so by creating a new merge commit that represents the combined history of both branches.

This method preserves the original commit history, showing all the branches involved in the development process. While merging can be beneficial for retaining context, it can also lead to a more complex commit history, making it challenging to trace changes.

The Importance of Frequent Rebase and Merge

Frequent rebasing and merging help ensure that team members stay in sync with each other's work. When done regularly, these processes mitigate risks associated with integrating changes from multiple developers. However, infrequent rebasing and merging can lead to a range of issues.

Increased Code Conflicts

One of the most significant risks of infrequent rebase and merge is the increased likelihood of code conflicts. When multiple developers work on the same codebase, changes can overlap, leading to situations where Git cannot automatically resolve which version of a line of code should be kept.

Example of Code Conflicts

Consider a scenario where two developers are working on the same file but in different branches. Developer A makes changes to a specific function and commits them to their branch. Meanwhile, Developer B also modifies that same function but has not yet merged their changes. If both developers delay rebasing or merging, when it comes time to integrate their work, Git will flag the file as having conflicts. This situation forces developers to spend time resolving conflicts, which can be frustrating and time-consuming.

Integration Issues

Infrequent rebasing and merging can lead to integration issues that compromise the stability of the project. When developers wait too long to integrate their changes, the differences between branches can become more pronounced, making it harder to reconcile them. This delay can result in a variety of problems, including:

Broken Builds: As changes accumulate in separate branches, the risk of introducing errors increases. When a developer finally merges their branch into the main branch, they may inadvertently break the build or introduce bugs that affect other parts of the application.

Compromised Functionality: New features developed in isolation may not function correctly when integrated with the rest of the codebase. Waiting too long to merge can lead to scenarios where critical functionality is lost or broken during integration.

Increased Complexity in the Codebase

As the codebase evolves, infrequent rebase and merge can lead to a more complex project structure. When developers avoid regular integration, the resulting commit history can become convoluted, making it challenging to understand the evolution of the project. A complex commit history can hinder the ability to track down bugs and understand the rationale behind design decisions.

Difficulty in Debugging: When a project has an extensive and tangled commit history, identifying the source of a bug can become increasingly difficult. Developers may spend excessive time sifting through commits to pinpoint where an issue was introduced.

Hindrance to Collaboration: A complicated codebase can deter collaboration among team members. New developers may find it challenging to navigate the project, which can lead to decreased productivity and hinder knowledge transfer.

Higher Costs in Development Time

Infrequent rebasing and merging can lead to increased development costs due to the time spent resolving conflicts and debugging integration issues.

When developers delay integrating their changes, they often find themselves facing a mountain of conflicts and complexities that could have been avoided with regular merging.

Time-Consuming Conflict Resolution: The longer developers wait to rebase or merge, the more conflicts they are likely to encounter. Resolving these conflicts can take hours or even days, diverting developers' attention from building new features or improving existing functionality.

Increased Testing Time: When integration occurs less frequently, more extensive testing is required to ensure that newly merged changes do not introduce new bugs. This increased testing can further prolong development timelines and increase costs.

Negative Impact on Team Morale

Frequent code conflicts and integration issues can lead to frustration and burnout among team members. Developers may feel overwhelmed by the challenges posed by infrequent rebasing and merging, leading to a decrease in morale and overall job satisfaction.

Frustration with Conflict Resolution: Constantly dealing with merge conflicts can become a source of frustration for developers, causing them to feel like they are constantly firefighting instead of making progress on their work.

Decreased Collaboration: When team members are reluctant to integrate their changes frequently, collaboration can suffer. Developers may become siloed in their work, missing opportunities for valuable input and feedback from their peers.

Conclusion

The risks and costs associated with infrequent rebase and merge in Git cannot be understated. From increased code conflicts and integration issues to higher development costs and negative impacts on team morale, the consequences of neglecting regular integration practices can significantly hinder the success of a software project.

To mitigate these risks, teams should prioritize frequent rebasing and merging as part of their development workflow. By establishing a culture of regular integration, teams can enhance collaboration, streamline the development process, and ultimately deliver higher-quality software. Investing in these practices not only leads to more successful projects but also fosters a more positive and productive team environment, ensuring that developers can focus on building innovative solutions rather than dealing with the fallout of infrequent integration.

The Case for Modern Code Editors: Why Software Developers Should Upgrade from Plain Text Editors

Efficiency and quality are paramount in the fast-evolving world of software development. Developers are constantly seeking tools that can enhance their workflow, streamline their processes, and ultimately improve the quality of the code they produce. While many experienced software programmers have honed their skills using plain text editors, the advent of modern code editors offers a wealth of features that can significantly elevate coding efficiency and code quality. In this article, we will explore the compelling reasons why developers should embrace modern code editors over traditional plain text editors, highlighting their advanced capabilities, including live linting, integrated development environments (IDEs), and artificial intelligence support.

The Evolution of Code Editors

From Plain Text to Modern Editors
Historically, plain text editors like Notepad or Vim have been the go-to choice for many developers, offering a simple and distraction-free interface for writing code.
These editors focus on the essentials, often lacking advanced features that boost productivity.

However, as software development practices have evolved and projects have grown more complex, the limitations of plain text editors have become increasingly evident.

Modern code editors such as Visual Studio Code, Atom, and Sublime Text have emerged as powerful alternatives, providing features like intelligent code completion, integrated debugging, and customizable extensions.

These tools not only streamline workflows but also help developers tackle the challenges of building sophisticated applications. As a result, the shift towards feature-rich editors reflects the changing demands of the industry and the need for more robust development environments.

Enhancing Code Quality

Real-Time Linting
One of the standout features of modern code editors is real-time linting. Traditional plain text editors require developers to write code and then run a separate linting process to check for errors and inconsistencies. This delay can lead to frustration and wasted time, especially in larger projects where debugging can be a cumbersome process.

In contrast, modern code editors provide local live linting, which immediately identifies syntax errors, code smells, and stylistic issues as the developer types. This immediate feedback allows developers to address issues on the fly, leading to cleaner and more robust code. For instance, if a developer makes a typo or uses a deprecated function, the code editor highlights the issue instantly, allowing for quick corrections before the code is even committed.

Code Formatting and Style Enforcement
Modern code editors often come with built-in formatting tools and support for popular style guides.

This feature ensures that code adheres to a consistent style, making it easier for teams to read and maintain the codebase. Automatic formatting on save means that developers can focus on writing code without worrying about whether their formatting is correct. This capability not only improves code readability but also fosters collaboration among team members who may have different coding styles.

Boosting Programming Efficiency

Integrated Development Environments (IDEs)

Many modern code editors are essentially lightweight IDEs, offering features such as debugging tools, integrated terminal support, and version control. These tools create a seamless development experience, enabling developers to manage their projects more efficiently without frequently switching between different applications. For instance, modern editors provide inline debugging capabilities, allowing developers to set breakpoints, inspect variables, and step through their code without leaving the editor.

This functionality reduces context-switching, which is often a significant drain on productivity, and helps developers stay focused on solving problems and writing high-quality code. Additionally, features like live collaboration and real-time code linting foster teamwork and ensure code consistency.

These editors are highly customizable, allowing developers to tailor their environments to specific workflows. As development processes become increasingly complex, the versatility of modern code editors makes them indispensable tools for improving both individual and team productivity.

Autocompletion and Intelligent Suggestions

One of the most significant advantages of modern code editors is their intelligent autocompletion features.

Traditional text editors offer basic keyword suggestions, but modern editors leverage advanced algorithms to provide context-aware code suggestions. This means that as developers type, the editor predicts what they intend to write and suggests relevant options based on the current context.

For instance, if a developer is working with a particular library or framework, the editor can provide suggestions for functions, parameters, and even usage examples, reducing the need to constantly consult documentation. This capability accelerates coding speed and reduces the cognitive load on developers, allowing them to focus on implementing logic rather than memorizing syntax.

Artificial Intelligence Assistance

The integration of artificial intelligence in modern code editors is a game-changer for software developers. AI-powered tools can analyze the code as it is being written and provide real-time feedback, suggestions, and even detect potential bugs before they occur. For instance, GitHub Copilot, an AI-powered code completion tool, can suggest entire lines or blocks of code based on the context of what the developer is working on.

This proactive assistance not only speeds up development but also helps developers learn best practices and discover new coding techniques. The AI can act as a mentor, guiding less experienced developers and providing seasoned developers with creative solutions they may not have considered.

Addressing Common Misconceptions

Experience vs. Tools
One common argument against adopting modern code editors is the belief that experienced developers can write high-quality code regardless of the tools they use. While it's true that experience plays a significant role in coding ability, it's essential to recognize that modern code editors can enhance even the most skilled developer's productivity.

Experienced developers can benefit from features like real-time linting and intelligent suggestions, which allow them to focus on complex logic rather than mundane tasks. By leveraging modern tools, developers can work more efficiently and produce higher-quality code, regardless of their level of expertise.

Overhead vs. Productivity
Another concern is that the additional features of modern code editors may introduce unnecessary overhead, potentially slowing down the development process.

However, the reality is that the benefits of using modern code editors far outweigh any minor performance impacts. The ability to catch errors early, streamline debugging, and leverage intelligent suggestions leads to a net gain in productivity, reducing the time spent on bug fixes and refactoring.

Conclusion

In a world where software development is becoming increasingly complex, the tools developers use to write code are more important than ever. While plain text editors have their place, modern code editors offer a wealth of features that enhance code quality, boost programming efficiency, and provide invaluable assistance through AI-driven capabilities.

By adopting modern code editors, software developers can significantly improve their workflows, reduce the time spent on debugging, and ultimately create higher-quality software. Embracing these powerful tools is not just a matter of convenience; it's an investment in the future of software development, ensuring that developers can navigate the challenges of modern programming with confidence and agility.

The Modern Software Architect: From Diagram Creator to Conductor of Collaboration

The role of the software architect has evolved significantly in recent years. Traditionally responsible for creating UML diagrams and detailed architectural blueprints, today's architect acts more like an orchestra conductor, guiding and harmonizing the development team's talents.

This article explores how the modern software architect has shifted from designing to leading, mentoring, and fostering collaboration among increasingly specialized software developers.

The Evolution of the Software Architect Role

From Design-Centric to Collaboration-Centric
In the past, software architects primarily focused on creating extensive documentation, including UML diagrams and technical specifications. Their success was often measured by the thoroughness of their designs and how closely the development team adhered to these documents. However, as software development has evolved into a more agile and collaborative discipline, the role of the architect has similarly evolved.

Today, the modern software architect is less about rigid documentation and more about facilitating communication and collaboration among team members. This shift is influenced by several factors:

Agile Development Practices: The adoption of Agile methodologies has placed greater emphasis on adaptability and iterative progress. Architects now work alongside developers, participating in sprints and stand-ups rather than working in isolation.

Diverse Skill Sets: Developers have become experts in specific libraries, frameworks, and programming languages. This specialization requires architects to shift their focus from technical details to architectural qualities and broader project goals.

Increased Complexity: As software systems become more complex, the need for collaboration across various roles, including developers, testers, and operations teams, has intensified. Architects now act as facilitators, helping to bridge gaps between different expertise.

The Architect as a Conductor

Guiding the Development Team

Just as an orchestra conductor leads musicians to create a harmonious performance, the modern software architect guides the development team in building high-quality software. This leadership role involves several key responsibilities:

Fostering Collaboration: The architect encourages open communication among team members, ensuring that developers feel comfortable sharing ideas and concerns. This collaborative environment fosters creativity and innovation, leading to better solutions.

Defining Architectural Qualities: Modern architects must prioritize architectural qualities, such as scalability, maintainability, and security. By understanding these qualities, architects can guide the team in making informed decisions that align with the project's long-term goals.

Mentoring Developers: Architects take on a mentorship role, sharing their knowledge and expertise with developers. This support helps developers deepen their understanding of architectural principles and best practices, ultimately improving the overall quality of the software.

Balancing Detail and Vision

While developers focus on the intricacies of coding, the architect's role is to maintain a high-level view of the project. This balance between detail and vision is crucial for successful software development. Key aspects of this balance include:

Understanding Technical Nuances: While the architect may not be as immersed in the day-to-day coding details, they must have a solid understanding of the technologies and frameworks being used. This knowledge enables architects to make informed decisions and provide valuable guidance to the development team.

Communicating the Vision: The architect is responsible for articulating the project's vision and objectives to the team. By providing clear direction, architects help developers understand how their work contributes to the broader goals of the project.

Navigating Trade-offs: Architects often face tough decisions regarding trade-offs between competing architectural qualities, such as performance and maintainability. Their ability to navigate these trade-offs while keeping the project's goals in mind is critical to its success.

Essential Qualities of the Modern Software Architect

To thrive in their evolving role, modern software architects must develop a unique set of skills and qualities:

Strong Communication Skills
Effective communication is paramount for architects. They must be able to convey complex ideas in a clear and understandable manner to various stakeholders, including developers, project managers, and clients. Architects should also actively listen to feedback and concerns, fostering an open dialogue within the team.

Empathy and Emotional Intelligence
Empathy allows architects to understand the perspectives and challenges faced by their team members. Emotional intelligence helps architects navigate team dynamics, addressing conflicts and fostering a positive work environment. This quality is particularly important in agile environments, where collaboration and adaptability are essential.

Deep Understanding of Architectural Qualities
Modern architects need a thorough understanding of architectural qualities such as:

Scalability: The ability to accommodate growing user demand without sacrificing performance.

Maintainability: The ease with which code can be modified and extended over time.

Security: Ensuring that the system is protected against vulnerabilities and threats.

Performance: Optimizing the system for speed and responsiveness.

By focusing on these qualities, architects can guide the development team toward creating software that meets both current and future needs.

Agile Mindset

An agile mindset is essential for modern architects, as it encourages flexibility and adaptability in response to changing requirements. Architects should embrace iterative development, be open to feedback, and be willing to pivot when necessary. This mindset helps architects align their work with the team's goals and the project's evolving needs.

Technical Competence

While the architect's focus may have shifted from coding to guiding, a solid technical foundation remains critical. Architects should stay current with industry trends, emerging technologies, and best practices. This knowledge allows them to provide informed guidance and support to the development team.

Conclusion

The modern software architect is no longer confined to the role of a diagram creator. Instead, they have evolved into a conductor, orchestrating the collaboration of diverse talents within the development team. By fostering communication, mentoring developers, and focusing on architectural qualities, architects play a crucial role in ensuring the success of software projects.

As software development continues to evolve, so too will the role of the architect. Embracing this transformation and adapting to the changing landscape will enable architects to lead their teams to success in an increasingly complex and dynamic world. By prioritizing collaboration, communication, and a focus on architectural qualities, modern architects can help shape the future of software development, ultimately creating high-quality solutions that meet the needs of users and stakeholders alike.

The Hidden Costs of Cultural Differences in Software Projects

In an increasingly globalized world, software development teams are often composed of members from diverse cultural backgrounds. While this diversity can lead to innovation and creativity, it also brings challenges that can significantly impact project costs. Cultural differences can create misunderstandings and misalignments, leading to increased expenses and lower quality outcomes. This article explores how cultural differences can escalate costs in software projects, illustrated with examples of common pitfalls.

Assumptions and Context

Cultural assumptions play a crucial role in communication and collaboration. What is considered common knowledge or implicit in one culture may not be understood the same way in another. For instance, in some cultures, direct communication is valued, and expectations are clearly stated. In contrast, other cultures may prioritize indirect communication, relying on context and non-verbal cues to convey meaning.

Example: Communication Styles

Imagine a scenario where a development team from a direct communication culture is working with a client from a more indirect communication culture. The development team assumes that all requirements and expectations are clear and unambiguous. However, the client may not express their concerns or preferences explicitly, believing that the team will intuitively understand their needs. This misalignment can lead to the team delivering a product that does not meet the client's expectations, resulting in costly rework and delays.

The Need for Clarity

In some cultures, certain topics are considered taboo or unnecessary to discuss openly, while in others, transparency and clarity are paramount. When working across cultures, it's essential to identify and articulate these differences to prevent misunderstandings.

Example: Defining Requirements

In a culture where assumptions are rarely questioned, a project manager might assume that a feature's functionality is understood without needing detailed specifications. On the other hand, a team member from a culture that emphasizes thorough documentation may feel uncomfortable proceeding without explicit instructions. As a result, the latter may end up spending unnecessary time seeking clarification or waiting for approval, leading to delays and increased costs.

Quality Expectations

Cultural differences can significantly influence perceptions of quality, as what is considered acceptable in one culture may not align with the standards of another. These variations can lead to misunderstandings, frustrations, and unexpected costs when adjustments are needed to meet the differing expectations. For example, a product that prioritizes functionality over aesthetics might be well-received in some regions, while others might place higher value on design and user experience. Similarly, communication styles and definitions of "completion" can vary, complicating collaboration across diverse teams. Addressing these cultural nuances early in the process is crucial to minimizing conflicts, ensuring alignment, and fostering better outcomes in global projects.

Example: Testing and Validation

Consider a situation where a development team in a high-context culture is accustomed to less rigorous testing processes because of a strong reliance on interpersonal relationships and trust.

In contrast, a client from a low-context culture may expect comprehensive testing and validation before any deliverables are accepted. If the team delivers a product that has not undergone thorough testing, the client may reject it, resulting in additional time and resources being spent to rectify the issues.

Increased Management Overhead
Cultural differences can necessitate additional layers of management to bridge the gaps in communication and understanding. This can lead to increased costs as more resources are allocated to ensure that everyone is on the same page.

Example: Coordination and Meetings
When teams from different cultures collaborate, it often requires more meetings and check-ins to ensure alignment. For instance, a software project involving team members from North America and Asia might require several meetings to discuss project goals, timelines, and expectations. Time zone differences can complicate scheduling, leading to inefficient use of time and increased project costs.

The Risk of Half-Delivers

Even with clear communication, cultural differences can result in deliverables that do not fully meet the client's expectations. This can happen when cultural-specific assumptions are missing, leading to misunderstandings about project goals and desired outcomes.

Example: Feature Set Misalignment
Suppose a team in a Western country is tasked with developing a software application for a client in an Eastern culture. The client may have specific features in mind that align with local customs and practices.

If these cultural nuances are not adequately communicated, the team might deliver a product with a feature set that does not resonate with the target audience, requiring further investment to revise the application.

Conclusion

Cultural differences in software development can significantly impact project costs, resulting in misunderstandings, misalignment, and ultimately, lower quality outcomes. By acknowledging and addressing these cultural nuances, teams can work more effectively and avoid costly pitfalls.

To mitigate the risks associated with cultural differences, organizations should prioritize clear communication, establish common ground, and invest in cultural competency training. Understanding the implications of cultural diversity can lead to more successful software projects, ultimately saving time and resources while enhancing the quality of deliverables. Embracing cultural differences as an asset rather than a liability can pave the way for innovative solutions and stronger collaborations in the software development landscape.

The Path to Successful Software Projects: Embracing Best Practices

The pressure to deliver high-quality projects on time can be overwhelming. However, by following a set of well-established best practices, teams can significantly increase their chances of success. This article will encourage you to embrace these strategies and remind you of the positive outcomes they can bring.

Embracing Collaboration and Communication
One of the most powerful ingredients for successful software projects is fostering a culture of collaboration and open communication.

When team members—developers, architects, and stakeholders—actively engage with one another, they create a strong foundation for understanding project goals and requirements. By encouraging open dialogue, you empower everyone to voice their ideas and concerns, leading to more innovative solutions and a cohesive team dynamic.

Clear Architectural Guidance
A modern software architect serves as a conductor, guiding the team towards a shared vision while emphasizing key architectural qualities such as scalability, maintainability, and security. By prioritizing these qualities, architects help developers make informed decisions and create robust solutions.

Remember, a clear architectural vision can significantly reduce confusion and improve the overall quality of the project.

Focusing on Quality and Continuous Improvement
Quality should be at the forefront of every software project. Implementing practices such as code reviews, real-time linting, and automated testing can drastically improve code quality and reduce bugs. By fostering a culture of continuous improvement, you encourage team members to learn from their mistakes and strive for excellence. This commitment to quality not only enhances the final product but also boosts team morale, as developers take pride in their work.

Adopting an Agile Mindset
An agile mindset allows teams to adapt quickly to changing requirements and respond to feedback in real time. Embracing agile principles fosters flexibility and encourages teams to break projects into smaller, manageable increments. This approach leads to more frequent releases, allowing teams to gather valuable user feedback and iterate on their solutions. By embracing agility, you position your project for long-term success.

Building Strong Documentation and Knowledge Sharing
While the modern architect may focus less on rigid documentation, the importance of maintaining clear architectural decisions and project documentation cannot be overstated.

Accessible documentation ensures that team members can ramp up quickly and that valuable knowledge is preserved. Encourage a culture of knowledge sharing, where everyone contributes to and learns from the documentation process. This practice strengthens the team's collective understanding and resilience, making it easier to onboard new members and maintain continuity.

Celebrating Small Wins

As you navigate the complexities of software development, it's essential to celebrate small wins along the way.

Acknowledging progress—whether it's completing a challenging feature, resolving a critical bug, or improving team collaboration—helps to maintain motivation and focus. Celebrations foster a positive atmosphere and remind the team of their shared goals, reinforcing the belief that success is within reach.

Conclusion

The path to successful software projects is paved with collaboration, clear architectural guidance, a commitment to quality, an agile mindset, and robust documentation practices. By embracing these principles, you can significantly increase your chances of delivering high-quality software that meets the needs of users and stakeholders alike.

So, gather your team, cultivate a spirit of collaboration, and embark on this journey together. Remember that every project is an opportunity for growth and learning, and with dedication and adherence to best practices, success is not just possible—it's within your reach. Let's make your next software project a resounding success!

Learnings from the titans

Tom DeMarco (Author, *Peopleware*):
"The most important thing in software development is not the tools, but the people who use them."

Steve Jobs (Co-founder, Apple):
"Design is not just what it looks like and feels like. Design is how it works."

Martin Fowler (Author, *Refactoring*):
"Any fool can write code that a computer can understand. Good programmers write code that humans can understand."

Linus Torvalds (Creator of Linux):
"Talk is cheap. Show me the code."

David Parnas (Software Engineer, Pioneer in Software Engineering):
"We cannot get architecture right by simply following a recipe; we have to understand the problem, and the design is a reflection of that understanding."

Michael Keeling (Author, *Software Architecture for Developers*):
"Software architecture is a complex set of decisions made to realize a system's requirements and goals."

James O. Coplien (Software Engineer, Author):
"Architecture isn't about making a pretty diagram, it's about designing a system that works and is scalable."